4/12/16

To "Lee & Don,"

Here's hoping this book
helps keep your fond
memories of "Downton Abbey"
alive! Love always,
Wally & Dick

Downton Abbey

A CELEBRATION

Downton Abbey
A CELEBRATION

By Jessica Fellowes
Foreword by Julian Fellowes

A Carnival Films / Masterpiece Co-production

Photography by Nick Briggs

St. Martin's Press ❧ New York

CONTENTS

CONTENTS

Foreword

BY JULIAN FELLOWES

So *Downton Abbey* is at last approaching touch–down, after six years on what has really felt at times like a magic carpet ride. We have taken a family, their servants and their friends, and tried to show how that world operated from before the Great War to the febrile 1920s, a curious time, with one foot among the Victorians and the other set firmly in the age of jazz and movies and air travel and, above all, change.

However much new frontiers were being reached by women like Edith, living lives that would have seemed incredible to their great grandmothers, it was still a world of tradition and it would not be until after the Second World War that the upper classes began to abandon the rules they had lived by since (what felt like) time immemorial. In this book, Jessica dissects their customs and habits, and tries to help us understand them. They were complicated, more complicated than they are generally allowed to be in fiction. They lived in splendour but with a sense of ordinariness. Pomposity and self-importance were not admired but nor was the abandonment of dignity. Things must be done correctly but not excessively, and this we have tried to demonstrate through the behaviour of Robert Grantham and his family. Most of these people derived much of their sense of identity from the house and the estate that they counted as their family seat. Many of them still do. Even when the house has gone, you will find paintings and engravings of it all around their homes and so Downton/Highclere has rightly been at the centre of everything. The point being that, whether or not we approve of it, this existence seems to give off a sense of security, which is perhaps one of the fundamental appeals of the show.

Of course their annual round was unshakeably divided into seasons, not just those of the calendar but the months allotted to sport and social activity. The Bible tells us there is a season for everything, which must be one of the few philosophies it shares with Burke's Peerage. Because there can be no question that, from long before this era, the notion that there was a right and a wrong way of doing things, and a right and a wrong time to do them, seems to have taken hold in every European society worthy of the name. While the activities and the days of the year they were practised may have varied, the concept is still with us today.

We have always made a great play of the clothes our characters wear, the men as well as the women, as the importance of dressing appropriately, for the date or the activity undertaken, was very much part of their sense of self. One of the giveaways of the 'outsider' was that he or she would be incorrectly dressed, and to find oneself wearing the wrong clothes, to arrive at a function wrongly kitted out, was everyone's worst nightmare. This has almost gone now because most of us hardly care, but it has only gone recently. As a child, I remember our very modest household was firmly steered by the notion that clothes must change at certain points of the year and these rules were closely observed. One of the cardinal crimes for my mother was the wearing of summer outfits before the correct season had been reached. She regarded the idea that a sunny day justified a summer dress as feeble in the extreme, and certainly my Scottish grandmother lived by the saying, 'Nay cast a clout 'til May is out' – although this always led to an argument as to whether it referred to the end of the month or the blooming of the may flower.

The London season still held mighty sway between the wars and, in the series, we have tried to show this, with both Sybil and Rose serving time as debutantes and being presented to the King, in Rose's case on screen. In those days, the June opening of the Summer

Adding insult to injury: Violet is serenaded by Martha at the indoor picnic.

from the hospital, the house found its metier during the war. Cora, particularly, relished the challenge of managing the officers and their needs, which brought her purpose and a sense of usefulness for the first time in her life. The fact was that for women of Cora's generation, if you were well-married and reasonably bright then that would be to your advantage – but it wouldn't translate into a career. Ladies' occupations before the war largely consisted of planning their wardrobe, a few charitable functions, checking with the cook and housekeeper that things were going to plan and fretting about their children's marital prospects. We may find this derisory now but it wasn't laziness or ineptitude that kept them stuck there – it would have been seen as socially, even morally, outrageous to consider doing anything else.

There were plenty who disagreed, of course, and the war gave many women a chance to change this, when they found themselves left behind to cope without their men who were at the front. This is seen in the detail of *Downton Abbey*: it was the work she did as a nurse that gave Sybil the strength to defy the expectations of her parents by marrying Branson. Edith learned that there was more than one way of going about life: she never stopped hoping she could marry and settle down to a more conventional life but so long as challenges were thrown at her, she continued to meet them. Indeed, by 1925, she positively relishes the power she holds as owner and publisher of a magazine with a London office. Mary was, perhaps, the least changed by the war itself but she certainly learned to embrace modern ideas as she headed into the 1920s. I doubt, for example, that she would have suggested that she work as the estate's agent before the war. We have seen both Edith and Mary leave the pleasures of embroidery behind to their mother's generation and move, as it were, out of the drawing room and into offices. Now, they have work to do.

Lady Mary Crawley
MICHELLE DOCKERY

Mary, as the eldest daughter of three sisters, grew up to feel a certain kind of guilt for not being a boy. It has made her tougher than most and created a determination to do right by the estate. This meant seeking a rich and powerful husband, one who would give her an important position in life; when we first met her, Mary was engaged to Patrick Crawley, Robert's heir. Not that she loved him – in fact, she was at times ruthless to a degree that even her grandmother felt she could do with a little softening of the heart. 'Mary's not above doing the wrong thing if she thinks that's what the moment calls for,' says Julian.

'I've always loved her complexity,' says Michelle Dockery. 'As a character, I'm always surprised by her. She's incredibly human – she can be as kind as she is mean. She goes to dark places and is always learning.' From the years 1912 to 1925, we've watched Mary grow from a girl to a woman: 'All that self-discovery,' says Michelle. 'When I first read the part, I thought she was a younger version of Lady Sylvia McCordle (the part played by Kristin Scott Thomas in *Gosford Park*). I wasn't expecting Mary to change, I thought she would remain mean and petulant. But she's evolved so much. She has those sides to her when she's trapped and cornered. I like it when she behaves badly – that's more interesting.'

For Michelle, the turning point in Mary's life was the death of Kemal Pamuk, of course. 'She began as quite an arrogant young girl,' she says. 'Mary was quite shaken and vulnerable after the incident. That vulnerability opened her up, and put her in touch with her emotions rather more.'

But it was also the love of Matthew that changed her. 'Mary presents a version of herself that is lovable for Matthew,' says Julian. He changes her and after his death, she feels that had he not, had she stayed as hard

as she was before, she might have been less unhappy. 'Mary certainly isn't a walkover,' says Michelle. 'She doesn't like to be told what to do. When she has an opinion about something, she won't back down... (But) Matthew brought out something in her she never knew she had.' Michelle loved her storyline with Matthew: 'When he was engaged (to Lavinia Swire) in series two, and then we had that pay-off at the end – she was at her most vulnerable. I did love series four because it was something I wasn't expecting and I had great stories. Mary was in a dark place and Carson was the one to bring her back to life.'

As often happened with the children of the house, she has a close relationship with Carson, as a long-

Mary's style has evolved dramatically over the six series.

Viewers loved watching the romance of Lady Mary and Matthew Crawley, with its eventual happy ending – so soon to be followed by tragedy.

standing servant and one that she probably spent quite a lot of time with as a young girl. 'He is another father figure to her, in a way,' says Michelle. 'When it comes to emotional matters she goes to Carson rather than to anyone else. She can be honest (with him).'

Mary's relationship with Edith is rather more complicated and, despite everything they have been through, has changed remarkably little from the antipathy they felt towards each other in the nursery. 'As much as Laura (Carmichael) and I find it fun because we're such good friends – we're always really excited when Julian writes a row between them – I often found it difficult because my relationship with my sisters is the complete opposite,' laughs Michelle.

In Anna, however, Mary has the relationship that she doesn't have with Edith. 'They grow really close – they're like sisters,' says Michelle. 'Mary's her true self around Anna. She's good at picking herself up and putting a face on when she needs to but with Anna she lets her guard down. She really cares what Anna thinks.'

The one person she does not seem to have had as good a relationship with as either might hope for is her mother. Cora's American background seems to be something that Mary treats as alien to her, rather than half her genetic make-up. 'She acts a little superior around her mother. She shows a sort of teenager's toughness that has never worn off,' says Michelle. 'She certainly isn't sentimental.'

Michelle has nothing but appreciation for what her work in *Downton Abbey* has brought her: 'There are so many things! I can't choose the best. Going to the Met Ball and discovering that actors you love, love your show. Taking my parents to Wimbledon, that was really special.'

Michelle is looking forward to life beyond Downton although she acknowledges that there is no magic ticket to her future success. Perhaps, rather fittingly, Michelle's favourite line reflects this, one that Carson says to Mary in the fifth series: 'We must always travel in hope.'

There's not much sisterly love between Mary and Edith.

Mary was dressed in this pale-coloured dress, while everyone else was in darker clothes, so she was the focal point.

MARY

Don't think I'm amused.
I really dislike my hand
being forced.

Footman Alfred serves Lady Rose from the left.

THE DINING ROOM

ROSE: I love cocktail parties.

CORA: Me, too. You only have to stay forty minutes, instead of sitting for seven courses, between a deaf landowner and an even deafer major general.

Eating is the cornerstone of life in a great house like Downton Abbey. While the family may have its duties to the estate and its villagers as employers and munificent landowners, it is in the dining room that they gather three times a day not just to eat but to hear news, discuss pressing matters, gossip and entertain their guests. For the servants, too, the mealtimes serve as the best demonstration of their skills, not to say their very raison d'être (at least where the cook and the butler are concerned). The cleaning of the silver and glass, the laying of the table, the preparing, cooking and serving of the food, the selection and pouring of the wine, the discreet positions they take standing around the room hearing, but never commenting upon, the conversation being conducted in front of them – all of these tasks are shared by the whole of the below stairs staff even if only the butler and the footmen are actually present during the meals themselves.

Because of these things, it is in the dining room that the traditions of the old way of life seem to have hung on the longest for the Crawleys. Dressing in white tie for dinner – an elaborate exercise that involved the entire family changing after Carson had rung the dressing gong – was still being observed by the family until after the First World War. This meant white ties and tailcoats for the men and full evening gowns for the women with tiaras in their hair. These are complicated and time-consuming to put on, as the hair has to be threaded through the bottom of the tiara, obscuring the cushion it sits on and making it appear to float on top of the head. In the fifth series, the family began to change into black tie, with evening dress but no tiaras for the women, when they had no guests, although they still changed into white tie if Violet was with them. When the dowager first saw Robert in black tie, she pretended to mistake her own son for a waiter, so appalled was she by his dress. But by the final series, set in 1925, only black tie is worn, even with Violet, and white tie is brought out only for very special occasions, such as when the Minister of Health, Neville Chamberlain, came to dinner.

Violet, of course, even when dining alone at the Dower House, continues to change into an evening dress and eat at her dining table, served by her butler. Isobel, who also lives alone, has quite a different outlook, as reflected by the fact that she stopped changing for dinner long ago and if she has no guests will happily eat off a tray in her drawing room. Such were the increments of change.

For Julian, writing the scripts, the value of the dining room as a location is that it provides the perfect opportunity for the whole family to gather and talk to each other, with the servants listening in – particularly the devious Thomas, who will use any tidbits he can for his own manipulative machinations. 'You're always looking for legitimate reasons to bring different characters into one place so you can get three or four stories progressed within one scene,' explains Julian. 'The advantage of the dining room is the presence of the footman and the butler, as well as the mechanics of what's going on beneath – you can have simultaneous actions for both halves of the drama. Sometimes, too, you want a long scene and the dining room gives you that in an unforced way, there's a kind of ballet of the servants going round the room. You never want too sedentary a scene but by definition the footman and the butler are always on the move.'

In this way, storylines introduced may then be discussed below stairs. For example, when Robert opens the morning paper and discovers, to his surprise, that his daughter Mary is engaged to Sir Richard Carlisle. That later becomes fuel for the servants' hall gossip. 'The audience is taking in little bits of information all the time, so they have to concentrate,' says Julian. 'With this kind of multi-narrative you can't go and make a cup of tea while you're watching. These group scenes keep the pace up with several storylines – having said that, then we'll take a scene in Mary's bedroom where we'll just have two of them talking about one thing. That feels quite refreshing as a lot of the scenes are short.'

At the dining table, too, Julian can bring new characters as guests and have them grilled by Violet. He can show how familiar they are with the rituals as a comment on their background – when Thomas patronisingly explained to Matthew that he could help himself, Matthew was quick to tell him he knew. And of course, it is an opportunity to bring up difficult topics of conversation to see how everyone copes, as was seen to particularly excruciating effect with Miss Sarah Bunting, the left-wing teacher friend of Tom's.

However, Julian concedes that he cannot write in too many scenes around the table as the actors would complain. Particularly Jim Carter, who must be on his feet for the ten to twelve hours it takes to shoot in that room. 'They're so dull to film! I do feel sorry for them,' says Julian, 'but I don't stop writing those scenes.' In real life as well as in the programme, the room is dominated by a vast van Dyck painting, an equestrian portrait of Charles I. The table itself appears proportionately rather small in the room but it has the advantage of bringing everyone together in a cosy, almost round-table fashion, as opposed to sitting at a huge banqueting table. The food stylist, Lisa Heathcote, must prepare some seventy-odd servings of the family's dinner in order to keep the food fresh upon the plates. And because the below stairs scenes are filmed on a set at Ealing Studios the food will have been carried out of the kitchens some weeks earlier, which means continuity has to be carefully checked. Continuity is a constant challenge when filming scenes in the dining room – after each take, the levels of wine in each glass, the amount of food on the plates and even the heights of the burning candles must be checked and altered. The table itself – which can be extended to just under fifteen feet, accommodating eighteen diners – belongs to Highclere Castle and is valuable, hence the white tablecloth that covers it, even though that is not strictly in keeping with the period. All the silver, Spode china and glass was bought by the props team at the start of filming.

At breakfast, the drama often begins with news brought to the table – whether it's a story in *The Times*, a telegram or a letter. In the very first episode, it saw the beginning of the Crawleys' central story: the sinking of the *Titanic*, which took the lives of Robert's heir and Mary's fiancé – their cousins, Patrick Crawley and his father, James. As breakfast is the most informal meal of the day – the family help themselves from chafing dishes on the sideboard – a little coming and going is easily written in. So when Robert read in silence the telegram Sybil had brought to him, he left immediately to see Cora in her bedroom, where she was eating her breakfast on a tray, as was the privilege of married women then. During the war,

At the dining table Bricker woos Cora, while
Miss Bunting shocks everyone with her views.

41

there were frequent letters bearing sad news, prompting Sybil to remark after one, 'It's as if all the men I ever danced with are dead,' a line taken from Julian's great aunt, Isie Stephenson, and her own sentiments in those terrible years.

Arriving at the breakfast table comes good news, too, even if not everyone feels the same way, as when Edith is first offered a job as a magazine columnist, the beginning of her story with Michael Gregson. Having Robert remark on stories in the newspaper is a handy way for Julian to tell the viewers what is going on in the real world at that time – news of the war, Lloyd George's policies, the new Labour government. Even Rose is spotted reading the paper from time to time, if not the more serious pages – it was over breakfast that she first showed her interest in the wireless radio.

The family serve themselves at breakfast. Married women take theirs upstairs, while Edith, as the only unmarried daughter, joins the men.

As all this shows, letters were the principal mode of communication even in 1925. While the telephone was increasingly used, it was still viewed as a rather serious and expensive mechanism. Also, there were few telephones in the house – one in the hall, the other in the butler's pantry – which meant that it was hard to have a private conversation. Telegrams were effective but necessarily brief. If you wanted to share gossip, worries or love with someone beyond the house, you did it by letter. The post was a very efficient system – there were two collections and two deliveries a day, meaning that a local invitation sent out by morning post could be replied to in the second post and received the following day. (In London, there were between six and twelve mail deliveries a day, making it possible for correspondents to write to each other several times in twenty-four hours.) The trouble with reading a letter at the breakfast table is that you have to do your best to conceal your feelings as you read it or everyone will start asking questions. This was something both family and servants endured, whether in the dining room or servants' hall.

Even after their substantial breakfast and with the prospect of a five-course dinner to come, luncheon would have been three courses and properly attended by the servants. We don't see many lunches at Downton Abbey as the dinners are dramatically more lively, with the women in their beautiful evening dresses and Julian being able to bring everyone around the table. At luncheon, it's more usual that one or two of the family at least will be elsewhere, whether busy on the estate or visiting someone locally. The most significant lunch scene we have had in the dining room was when Mary decided to join the tenants' lunch, an annual event at the house. It marked the moment she decided to end her period of mourning for Matthew and join the land of the living once more. We also saw Ethel interrupt lunch with the Bryants to show them their grandson, Charlie, and in the sixth series guest Mrs Harding surprises the servants when she turns out to be a familiar face.

But it's the grandeur and formality of the evening dinners at Downton Abbey that provide the best scope for dramatic tension. You would think that comfort would be drawn from the fact that everyone is gathered in their finery, eating off the house's best china, drinking carefully chosen wine out of delicately etched glasses and observing the rules and rituals that have been carried out for at least a hundred years. For Violet, at least, these dinners would be a welcome respite from the churning, often bewildering, changes that rampaged in the world beyond those walls. Here, she could pretend that life was just as she had always known it. But of course it is precisely in those situations – where one would like everything to be *just so* – that the scene is perfectly set for everything to go wrong.

MRS HUGHES

I'm changing round the dessert services. We always seem to use the Meissen and never the Spode.

The Crawleys entertain lunch guests Mr and Mrs Harding.
The crew set up the scene, with Michelle Dockery keeping
warm in the meantime.

For a start, even Downton Abbey can't batten down the hatches against modern life altogether as the younger members of the family insist on bringing their new ideas and provocative conversation to the table. Sometimes it's someone from the older generation – Isobel particularly seems to enjoy throwing a bomb into the proceedings at dinner and Cora's mother, Martha Levinson, delights in the chance to send Violet into paroxysms over the soup.

Much to Carson's dismay, the servants let the side down occasionally – as when Mrs Patmore put salt on the meringues instead of sugar. Or when, during the war, things got so bad with all the male servants away, housemaids had to serve. Indelibly inked on Carson's list of Terrible Times is surely the moment when Branson was still a chauffeur and he volunteered to help as footman for a particularly smart dinner with a visiting general. Only at the last minute did Carson become aware that Branson was planning a dastardly deed at the dinner table, and intervened just in time, grappling him down the stairs. In filming this scene, Allen Leech remembers that he and Jim Carter encountered a problem – they filmed Carson grappling Branson from the dining room and through the green baize door to take him below stairs, out of harm's way. But when they came to film the second half of the scene – coming down the stairs and into the servants' hall – it was several weeks later at Ealing Studios and neither of them could remember whether Jim's left hand had been on Allen's collar or on his waist! Luckily the continuity script supervisor was at hand.

At the back of the dining room, partly hidden by a screen (provided by the props department), is the servery. This is where the glasses are kept and where Carson will carve the meat. Fortunately, the dining room is only a short flight of stairs and little passageway from the kitchen, which means the food arrives still hot. When designing these houses, architects were mindful of keeping cooking smells from drifting into the state rooms, which could mean kitchens were placed very far away. Arthur Inch, the butler that advised Julian on *Gosford Park*, said that when he worked at Blenheim Palace, the dining room was almost a quarter of a mile away from the kitchens. No wonder that a former Duke of Marlborough was said to have complained that he had never had a hot meal at Blenheim.

Mrs Patmore would cook as many as five courses for dinner, seven for a very grand occasion. Throughout the sixth series the same rituals were observed. Carson pours the wine, while the footmen serve the food – this being the only time you see them wear white gloves, so as not to leave fingerprints on the plates. Food is always served and taken away from the left, drinks from the right, and the footmen serve with one seat between them so as to avoid any bumping. Robert sits at the head of the table for breakfast but, at lunch and dinner, he and Cora sit opposite each other in the middle of the longer sides, as the Royals do. Food is served 'à la russe', with everyone helping themselves from platters that the footmen carry round, starting with the woman on Robert's right and continuing one by one. It's only on the Continent that women are served first and as Anna remarks, 'We don't like foreign ways here.' Second helpings are never offered – there's quite enough food with five or more courses, though portions were not large. Once the supper is over, Cora and the women 'split', leaving the dining room to have coffee in the drawing room, while the men stay behind to drink port. Robert tries not to linger too long because it is only once he has left to join the women that the footmen, with the help of the housemaids, can clear the table and then go downstairs to have their own supper. Of course, sometimes, if alone, Robert does not wish to stay behind at all.

It was this time at the table that gave Robert his opportunity for man-to-man talks. It would have been in these moments that he would have got to know Matthew and Tom better, as they relaxed and sat back after dinner. Indeed, it could be crucial for him in sounding out his daughters' suitors, giving him a real chance to find out for himself exactly what he thought of them. It was, in fact, over the port that Robert decided once and for all that he would not try to fight the entail and make his daughter heiress of the estate. Only at this stage of the dinner did the Duke of Crowborough, whom everyone expected to ask Mary to marry him, reveal himself to be a fortune hunter. Despite the fact that Robert himself had been the same, marrying Cora for her father's American riches to save Downton, he felt he could not risk the same kind of marriage for his daughter. As he points out to Cora, he is 'so much nicer' than the duke. Robert showed a clear head then but perhaps less so when he kissed the housemaid, Jane, in the servery. Oh dear.

One of the most memorable scenes in the dining room was a romantic one – when Matthew and Mary first kissed. In the lead-up to this long-awaited moment, Matthew had come to Sybil's rescue, along with Branson, after she was injured by the thuggish crowd waiting to hear the results of the Ripon by-election. She was taken back to Crawley House, where Isobel cleaned her head wound and sent her back to the Abbey. By then, it was late and Matthew had missed supper so Mary asked if some sandwiches could be brought up to the dining room for him. The two of them sat alone together. They had been, by this point, skirting around each other for some time with mixed messages flying about – Matthew thought Mary liked Strallan; Mary thought Matthew could like Sybil. At last, he poured her a glass of wine and poured another for himself in the water glass – it amused her that Matthew did not need to be fastidious about getting things right. She asked him if when he flirted and laughed with her he did it out of duty. He reminded her that she had said some choice things about him when he first arrived, two years before. 'Oh, Matthew,' she replied. 'What am I always telling you? You must pay no attention to the things I say.' And then – they kissed. And all the viewers heaved a sigh of relief.

VIOLET
The system has worked well here for a hundred years. Why must we destroy everything in our paths, simply for the sake of change?

CLARKSON
I'm not sure that's a true representation of the case.

Violet invites the Minister of Health, Neville Chamberlain, to dinner during the battle over the hospital.

The Earl of Grantham
HUGH BONNEVILLE

Robert, the 5th Earl of Grantham, is in many ways forced to deal with a changing world. Born into the Victorian era to a dominant mother and a father about whom we know little except that he was a product of his era, Robert was brought up with the expectation that he would live a life exactly like his forebears. As an earl-in-waiting he enjoyed the privileges accorded to him, whether his Eton education, his European travels, the servants attending him, the house and estate in which he grew up and expected to die in, the deference paid to him by others – without ever questioning the wrongs or rights of this. As Julian says of Robert: 'He thinks it's fine he's a squillionaire earl living like a Renaissance prince, so long as he's polite to the servants and nice to his tenants.' Despite all the many changes that he endures, 'Robert's morality never changes,' says Julian. 'He thinks a pyramid society is good for the nation. He has no objection to new money and people coming up, he's happy about social mobility. But he's not happy about the collapsing of the permanences. What marks that generation, and the ones before them, from now is that they were so unquestioning. My father was born into a landed gentry family with a degree of social perks, if no money, and he thought neither of who was below and who was above. If he met a very stupid duke, he wouldn't think it was ridiculous that the duke was above him – it just wouldn't be a relevant factor. And I think Robert is the same. Nor would they think – by what right am I sitting here at the Ritz, as opposed to sitting in Neasden counting every penny? That belief in a stable society at the core was their model.'

> **CORA**
> *Heavens. Papa's conversion to the modern world is almost complete.*
>
> **EDITH**
> *Don't be deceived. He'd still like to see us happy wives and mothers, admit it?*

When asked if he shares any qualities with Robert, Hugh Bonneville is quick to reply: 'I'm around six foot two inches and talk exactly like Robert. I'd like to think I also share his tolerance and sense of fair play.' Of course, between an earl of 1925 and an actor of 2015, there is a key difference: 'My sole purpose in life is not the maintenance of a huge estate and I don't hunt, shoot or fish. I'd like to think I'm a bit more perceptive about what's going on under my nose than sometimes he is.'

Robert with one of his beloved labradors, Pharaoh.

As an earl, it is essential that Robert has the correct attire for every occasion, be it dinner, hunting or inspecting his estate.

Robert is a simple man encoutering an increasingly complicated world. 'He is by nature a conservative with a small "c",' says Hugh. 'He doesn't want change, he just wants to conserve Downton Abbey. But of course everything is changing all the time and he gets carried along by it.'

After the war – during which Robert felt about as useful as a chocolate teapot – it took a while for him to regain a sense of purpose. Hugh blames that dose of the 'black dog' for Robert going off the rails morally (as when he kissed the maid, Jane). And things didn't improve for a while: 'His hopes that after the war things will return to normal are constantly disappointed.'

One thinks of the female cast as having the most to contend with when it comes to costumes, particularly in the early series when they were all required to wear corsets. But even Hugh had a reason to embrace the more relaxed fashions of the 1920s, when white tie was worn more rarely: 'The worst was the white tie – beautifully made by Huntsman of Savile Row – it's the stiff shirt fronts and starched collars that slice into your neck that make you feel as if you're in a straitjacket.'

Robert is invigorated by his children. 'He does in fact have quite liberal tendencies,' says Hugh. 'He always makes a token gesture of disapproving of his daughters' decisions. But he secretly approves of them ploughing their own furrows. If he tries to intervene in their lives, it is always because he wants the best for them.' Robert's love for his children has grown over the series, perhaps as he has realised that they are coping better in the modern world than he is – he increasingly respects and admires the choices they make, managing to reverse his own rather more Victorian views as a result. We see this most clearly as he learns to take Mary's decisions on the estate seriously and when he accepts Marigold as Edith's daughter. Sadly, it may have been the death of his beloved Sybil that taught Robert to hold on to his family above all else.

Apart from his wife and daughters, Robert's closest relationship is with Bates, something Hugh has enjoyed: 'I have always liked the relationship between Robert and Bates, particularly in the first two series,' he says. 'In terms of plot, I enjoyed Mr Bricker's effect on Robert and Cora's equilibrium. Robert was fantastically dim about the art historian's intentions, which was fun to play.'

Most of all, Hugh has thoroughly enjoyed and admired the work on the show: 'Everyone on the programme is working at the very top of their game, which is something very special. It creates a great support network.' That said, he is clear about who his best friend on set is: 'The director of photography. Always the director of photography.'

Robert's marriage to Cora may have begun as an expediency, but their love for each other after thirty-five years is clear.

Robert in his Savile Row tailored white tie.

ROBERT

You see a million bricks
that may crumble...
I see my life's work.

Punch and Judy are Downton Abbey's own box-set entertainment.

THE LIBRARY

BRANSON: *This is our sitting room, really.*
The drawing room's more formal. This is for tea
or writing letters, or anything like that.

*D*espite its imposing size, book-lined walls, gold columns, ornate ceiling and gigantic rugs, the library is perhaps the cosiest, least formal of all the state rooms. This is because it is Victorian club room architecture of the best variety – full of 'rich plumpness and masculine opulence' according to *Country Life*; it was decorated by Thomas Allom, who had completed the hall after George Barry's death. This makes it perfect for the master of the house. More than 5,600 books line the walls, some dating back to the sixteenth century. Dusty tomes and bright comedies, doubtless *The Complete Works of Shakespeare*, not to mention volumes of poetry by those that have loved and lost, all sit on the shelves waiting to be read.

At Downton Abbey, the library acts as Robert's study during the day and is where he will hold his meetings with the agent or his lawyer, Murray. It was here that Robert had the fateful conversation with Murray in which his lawyer had the thorny task of telling him that he had lost his entire fortune in a single bad investment, the Canadian Grand Trunk Line (a real-life disaster).

If Robert needs to formally discuss anything with a servant, he'll call them to a meeting by his desk – such as when he told a shocked Mrs Patmore that he had arranged for her to have an eye operation in London. In here, we also saw Robert ask Sir Anthony Strallan to stay away from Edith – a request which was understood by the older, crippled Strallan then, if not later. In latter years, Robert pours himself some whisky before supper in the library – not a development with which Carson is entirely happy. This reluctance to let go of the traditional formalities is with Carson even when he is supposed to be off duty. Remember his discomfort when Mrs Hughes invited him to sit down in the library when the family was away? A servant would *never* be seated in the presence of the family, even below stairs, and in the many years he had worked at Downton, this would have been the only time Carson sat on state room furniture.

Carson and Mrs Hughes each have a quite different reaction to their stolen moment sitting down in the library.

Overlooking the drive at the front of the house, with the lawn sweeping behind it, the library is where some of the family's most intimate moments have taken place. This is because it is the room in which the family gathers at the least formal time of day – teatime. In the late afternoon, when the fire has been lit, whoever is in the house gathers for a cup of tea and a slice of cake (eaten with fingers, never with forks) and we even see Sybbie, George and Marigold come down to join their parents for their daily hour by the fire. Wearing day clothes, away from the formalities of dinner table etiquette, and without any servants standing in the background to listen in, they are free to discuss their worries or hopes openly. (Well, as openly as they discussed anything in 1925.) Such as when Lady Rose read in the newspaper about a nudist colony opening in Essex ('rather damp,' was Violet's dry response), or when Robert was in misery over the Labour government coming to power.

Which is not to say the room hasn't seen its dramatic moments – it was here, when Lavinia tripped on a rug and threatened to fall headlong into the fire, that Matthew suddenly stood up from his wheelchair to save her, after he believed he might never walk again.

Matthew discovers he can walk again, to his and fiancée Lavinia's delight.

The family gather in the large library to discuss Edith's disappearance. The small library can be seen behind the columns of the archway. These rooms are largely unchanged by the art department for the set.

VIOLET

The library was assembled by the fourth Earl. He loved books.

MARY

What else did he collect?

VIOLET

Horses and women.

It is rare for Mrs Patmore to be summoned above stairs.

In 1925 there were exciting new books published, although one can't guarantee that these modern titles would have found a place amongst Robert's leather-bound collection. Robert has a ledger in which everyone must write down the book they have borrowed – in this way, he is able to keep a close eye on their tastes and ensure they return them. I like to imagine Mary enjoying F. Scott Fitzgerald's tale of the louche rich in *The Great Gatsby*. Cora might further her investigations into the absurdities of the English aristocracy with P. G. Wodehouse's *Carry On, Jeeves*. And can't one rather fancy that Edith would have been a fan of Virginia Woolf's *Mrs Dalloway*? After all, she'd met the famous writer once, in Michael Gregson's flat, when he was still alive.

The servants, too, are invited to borrow books although only the more senior ones will feel that it is within their right to do so. Robert is unlikely to be surprised by Carson's choices – historical biographies of notable European kings and queens, for the most part. Carson is not the sort of man to choose a book that challenges his views. Mrs Hughes, one supposes, will select the novels of Jane Austen and Charlotte Brontë; one wouldn't describe her as a romantic, exactly, but it's clear she can be moved by matters of the heart. Mrs Patmore wouldn't have the nerve to come up the stairs to browse the library and anyway, if her nose gets stuck in a book it's more likely to be *Mrs Beeton's Book of Household Management* or the Bible, which she is fond of quoting from. Perhaps Anna and Bates might read *The Trial* by Franz Kafka, also published in 1925, although it could be just a little too close to home. They might prefer a Sherlock Holmes adventure by Arthur Conan Doyle instead.

But it was Tom Branson's interest in books that really told a story of its own. We first met Branson in the library, when he came to introduce himself to Robert on his first day of work. Arriving as a chauffeur, he had the post of a senior, slightly separate servant. Chauffeurs were regarded in much the same light as grooms, and as grooms were given quarters close to the horses they looked after,

Robert deals with the chambermaid from the
Grand Hotel in Liverpool, who tries to blackmail
Mary about her stay there with Lord Gillingham.

chauffeurs were kept by the cars. So they had their own lodgings by the stables, where they would eat separately from the other servants and could even live with a wife and children, should they have them. They were considered skilled and knowledgeable – cars being then still a thing of mystery – as chauffeurs were also competent mechanics. All of which meant that Robert was pleasant to the new young man in the household and naturally took more interest in him than he would in, say, a new footman.

We first got an indication of Branson's radical ideas in that meeting with Robert. Branson admired the library and impressed his new employer when he said he'd like to borrow books. Robert was made a little nervous when the chauffeur told him that he liked to read Karl Marx and other left-wing writers and felt later that his point was only proved.

Later, it is of course Branson's radical politics that prove to be so attractive to Sybil and in this same room she fought back with such spirit against her parents' disapproval of her romantic alliance.

The library itself is actually two rooms, divided by an open archway with two golden columns. There is a larger and a smaller library on either side. During the war, the larger library became a place of recreation for the convalescing officers, with a ping-pong table, card tables, an upright piano and so on. This meant that the smaller library could be kept for the family's use and also gave Julian a dramatic advantage in writing the scenes, as neither room was completely hidden from the other. On the officers' side of the room we had two short-lived romances developing – that between the luckless housemaid Ethel and Major Bryant (she became pregnant and gave the child, Charlie, to his parents to bring up after Major Bryant was killed in one of the war's last offensives) and 'Patrick Crawley' supposedly back from the dead as a Canadian, who stole Edith's heart.

Perhaps the most extraordinary romantic encounter was in here too when the exiled Russian, Prince Kuragin, recognised his former love, Violet. It was not, it is fair to say, a story that anyone was expecting.

As the room that best operates as a place of work during the day, the library has also been used for police interviews – most notably when Anna was questioned over the death of Mr Green. In here, too, Mr Grigg confronted Robert over Carson, hoping to blackmail him out of a large sum – he failed but not before we had all been merrily told the revelation that Carson had once been one half of the music hall act, The Cheerful Charlies. Strangely enough, the telephone for the house is

> SYBIL
>
> *Your threats are hollow, don't you see? I won't be received in London, I won't be welcome at Court. How do I make you understand? I couldn't care less.*

MRS HUGHES

There seems to be a good deal of emotion being vented among the guests in the library. But then they are foreigners.

When Robert invites a group of Russian refugees to Downton Abbey, Prince Kuragin and Violet recognise each other after more than fifty years.

A final farewell to Isis, before she is carried upstairs to lie with Robert and Cora.

not on Robert's desk but in the hall, meaning all calls could be easily overheard, such as Edith arguing with Mr Skinner, the editor of her magazine, *The Sketch*.

From the libraries, the bell would be rung quite frequently, calling Carson or a footman to bring tea, clear tea, or put more wood on the fire. A footman would never knock on the door – he would simply appear, because the bell had been sounded. Molesley would pour the tea and hand out slices of cake while the children looked at books or worked on a jigsaw puzzle. In one scene from the final series, all of the parents are away, so Granny and 'Donk' laid out books about the Egyptians (a nod to the Carnarvon history here, in which the 4th Earl discovered Tutunkhamen's tomb with Howard Carter and also the reason the dogs were named Pharaoh and Isis) for George, Sybbie and Marigold to look at.

Before shooting this scene with the children there was a crew rehearsal, a process witnessed by about fifty people standing around the room – the technicians watch to see where the actors move, which helps them understand where the cameras will go, what lighting is needed, where the sound boom must move to and so on. Elizabeth McGovern was in costume but the house was cold even on a mild spring day, so she wore a fluffy pink dressing-gown over the top of her clothes and Ugg boots on her feet. The young actors' parents watched slightly anxiously in the background, motioning to their child if he or she needed to look in a different direction. When filming started, there were the inevitable breaks between takes so Hugh Bonneville and Elizabeth took the opportunity to reassure the children, and it was clear their charges were relaxed and happy, enjoying the task in hand. A perfectly Downton-esque atmosphere.

Sybbie, George and Marigold

FIFI HART, OLIVER AND ZAC BARKER, EVA AND KARINA SAMMS

For quite a long time, there were no children at Downton Abbey. This always rather saddened Julian who was keen to write in the stories of footmen who carried children piggy-back in the hallways, and cooks that slipped them treats, as many memoirs of the period recall. But the jumps in time of the first two series (from 1912–1914, then 1916–1919) meant that it was an impractical idea from a casting point of view – the children would have had to be recast several times within two series. But once the third series began and the time periods slowed down, it started to be possible. So now, in 1925, for the sixth and final series, there are three children – and Thomas has often been found giving one or two of them a piggy-back ride. Master George, the son of Mary and the late Matthew; Miss Sybbie, daughter of Tom and the late Sybil; and Miss Marigold, daughter of Edith and the late Michael Gregson.

All near to each other in age and each sharing the loss of one parent, they are as close as siblings. But although they are adored by their parents and the family around them, not to mention by the servants, they are being brought up as aristocratic children were in the 1920s – that is to say, by nannies and largely out of sight. The children sleep, eat and play in the nursery, which is on the floor above the family bedrooms, off the servants' back stairs and behind a green baize door. In fact, the nursery as we see it on the screen is Robert's dressing room repainted and dressed on set at Ealing Studios. Once a day, at teatime, the children are dressed in clean, starched clothes and brought down to the library to spend an hour or so with their parents, Granny and 'Donk'. Robert's not keen on the nickname given to him by Sybbie after they played a game of 'Pin the tail on the donkey' – but it seems he's stuck with it now. Tom, who better remembers his childhood in Ireland, seems more inclined to take Sybbie off for walks by himself.

The children have all been played by the same actors in series five and six, having aged in real life at the exact same rate as their characters. The oldest child, Sybbie, is played by Fifi Hart, but the other two are each played by twins. Marigold by Eva and Karina Samms; George by Oliver and Zac Barker. This is so that if one child is not feeling on form, the twin will be available instead; it also prevents too long working hours for a child. Scenes that feature the children are short but it is, says executive producer Liz Trubridge, 'nigh on impossible to predict how long the rehearsals will take with unexpected problems on the day, overrunning of scenes etc. So we give ourselves maximum flexibility and also ensure the children have proper rest time, eating time and play time.' Like most things, it's not a foolproof system – as when Oliver and Zac turned up to film one scene and one brother had a cut on his chin, while the other did not. In the sixth series as the children have grown a little older – they are now between two and five years old – and can talk, Julian has written in more interaction between them and the servants.

> **ROSAMUND**
> *And how would we execute this insanity? A farmer's foster child turns up in the Downton nursery?*
>
> **EDITH**
> *People adopt babies all the time, from all kinds of backgrounds.*

Cousins Marigold, Sybbie and George live together at Downton as brothers and sisters would.

Cora's bedroom is where she takes her breakfast and receives her post.

LORD & LADY GRANTHAM'S ROOMS

CORA: *I can't believe it.*

ROBERT: *I can. Sneaking off like a thief in the night.*
That's O'Brien to a T.

Cora's day begins and ends in her bedroom as you might expect, but perhaps what is more unusual is that this room is the focus of not one but two important relationships in her life. So long as they are not in the midst of an argument, when he is banished to his dressing room, then her husband is the person Cora sees first and last. But this is only very shortly before and after she has seen her lady's maid.

Following the sudden departure of O'Brien and the equally swift farewell to Braithwaite, Cora is now happily settled with Baxter, her lady's maid since halfway through the fourth series. Baxter has had a chequered past but is not a woman to make excuses for herself, and Cora, as a liberal employer, is willing to have faith that her lady's maid has turned over a new leaf. With someone so closely by you in your most intimate of spaces, it's crucial that a mistress has complete trust in her maid.

Not long before eight o'clock in the morning, Robert will have kissed his wife and left for his dressing room before going downstairs for breakfast. As a married woman, Cora enjoys the privilege of rising a little later. Baxter will come in and draw the curtains before placing her tray on the bed. A glass of fresh orange juice, an occasional nice touch by Baxter to remind Cora of her American background, a small pot of tea, some toast, perhaps an egg. And on the tray too, a copy of the *Daily Sketch* or *Woman's Weekly*, plus any letters that have arrived.

Each item on the tray has been put together by the art department and while it may flash by on our small screens, careful attention is paid to each. The food is all real, prepared by food stylist Lisa Heathcote – even the egg is cooked. The newspaper will be an exact facsimile of one from the period and the letters will have been created specially; each one written on the correct paper for the era, by either a man or woman as appropriate, using a fountain pen and ink and even containing the right sentiments.

While Cora apprises herself of the latest news, Baxter will be busy putting out her mistress's clothes for the day. This bedroom is her place of work above stairs and while Cora is reading the papers or in her bath, Baxter will be checking Cora's dresses, thinking ahead to the next few days. Does anything need cleaning, ironing or mending?

Shoes would be taken down to the boot room to be cleaned. Most items would be sent to the laundry on the estate but more delicate silks and evening dresses would be washed by Baxter, by hand. The lady's maid liked to exert complete control over her mistress's domain. Quite often, ladies' maids would be the ones to dust the dressing table, preferring not to leave it to the hands of the housemaids.

Cora's bedroom is a copy of the blue Mercia bedroom at Highclere (which has been redecorated since the first series was filmed), with its eighteenth-century four-poster bed and silk hangings. The room is south facing and overlooks the arch of the folly, Heaven's Gate. Cora's dressing table sits between the two large windows of the room, with an oval mirror and two small lamps. Baxter would manage the jewellery, seeing what needs cleaning and keeping anything that is not to be worn in the safe, taking out what is needed in advance. She'd prepare in here for any travelling – packing suitcases carefully. Ladies' maids would be expected to anticipate their mistress's needs, even planning their wardrobe for them. The ladies' maids would travel with their mistresses, too, which gave them a different life as a servant, quite used to travelling to London and so on. Anna had the opportunity of travelling to Scotland for the first time in her life, as well as to France for Mary's honeymoon. O'Brien seized her chance to work in India, and really see a different world to the one she was used to. But more usually ladies' maids would travel with their mistresses to other grand houses in Britain, just as Baxter accompanies Cora to Brancaster Castle.

In this way, a lady's maid came to understand and see much of other servants' households and in the process would become very well informed on how things were done elsewhere. It also meant they had their ears close to the ground, hearing when jobs were becoming available or finding out who was and wasn't a good employer. Equally, mistresses would grill their maids for the below stairs gossip in other houses.

Not being dressed in a uniform, some ladies' maids might be easily mistaken for a guest in another house. The Hon. Mrs John Mildmay White told a story of going to a house in Shropshire for the first time when 'my maid, who was very pretty, found herself in the drawing room, while I found myself in the back regions. She looked so much better than I did!'

BAXTER

What would you like to wear m'lady?

CORA

Well, I don't want to insult them.
I should look as though I've tried…

BAXTER

Elegant but sensible. I know.

Cora with her lady's maids: Braithwaite, O'Brien and Baxter.

Having servants around all the time certainly made daily life jolly easy – but some didn't enjoy it. Lady Mander, chatelaine of Wightwick, found that her later years with fewer servants were 'a relief… not to have to try to keep up appearances or guard one's speech at meals or to catch hostile glances from the gardener for picking a flower instead of waiting for him to bring plants in from the hothouse'. The most shocking incident of this nature – that is, a hostile servant – at Downton Abbey was the moment O'Brien decided to leave half a bar of soap on the floor by Cora's bath. Almost as soon as she had done it, she regretted it… but it was too late. The pregnant Cora slipped, fell and in doing so, lost her delightfully unexpected, longed-for son. The sorrow at what she had done almost drove O'Brien mad – consequently she became fiercely overprotective of her mistress and, ironically, ended up saving her life when she nursed her through the worst of the Spanish flu.

INT. CORA'S BEDROOM. DOWNTON. DAY. Cora enters and stops dead. Some embroidered evening coats are strewn on the bed and Mrs Hughes is wearing one over the mail-order dress. Mrs Patmore and Anna are with her.

In the sixth series, Cora had a shock when she came into her room to find the servants – Anna, Mrs Patmore and Mrs Hughes – pulling her evening coats out of the wardrobe and even wearing one. She jumped to a mistaken conclusion but at least, being Cora, she was quick to put it right.

Cora's bedroom is also, of course, the place where she sleeps with Robert every night although it is always referred to as *her* bedroom, never as *their* bedroom. This is because it was considered much smarter to sleep in separate beds. There's something rather intriguing, as a viewer, about hearing the pillow talk of this couple we have grown to know so well. There's no doubt they love each other but over thirty-five years or so of marriage, there have been downs as well as ups. On the whole, they share their difficulties and comfort each other. In this room, Robert first told Cora of the death of his cousin and heir, Patrick Crawley. Later, he confessed that he lost all the money of the estate, most of which was hers. (A resilient type, Cora's response was both typical and refreshing – 'I'm an American – have gun, will travel.') And most touching of all – certainly as far as the viewers were concerned – was the night that Robert brought his beloved dog, Isis, to their bed as she died.

But there have been some moments of fury, too – as the night Robert came home, unexpectedly, to find Simon Bricker standing in his wife's room, both of them wearing their dressing gowns. You can see why he leapt to the wrong conclusion. I don't think there were many who didn't cheer at Robert's landing a punch on Bricker's jaw.

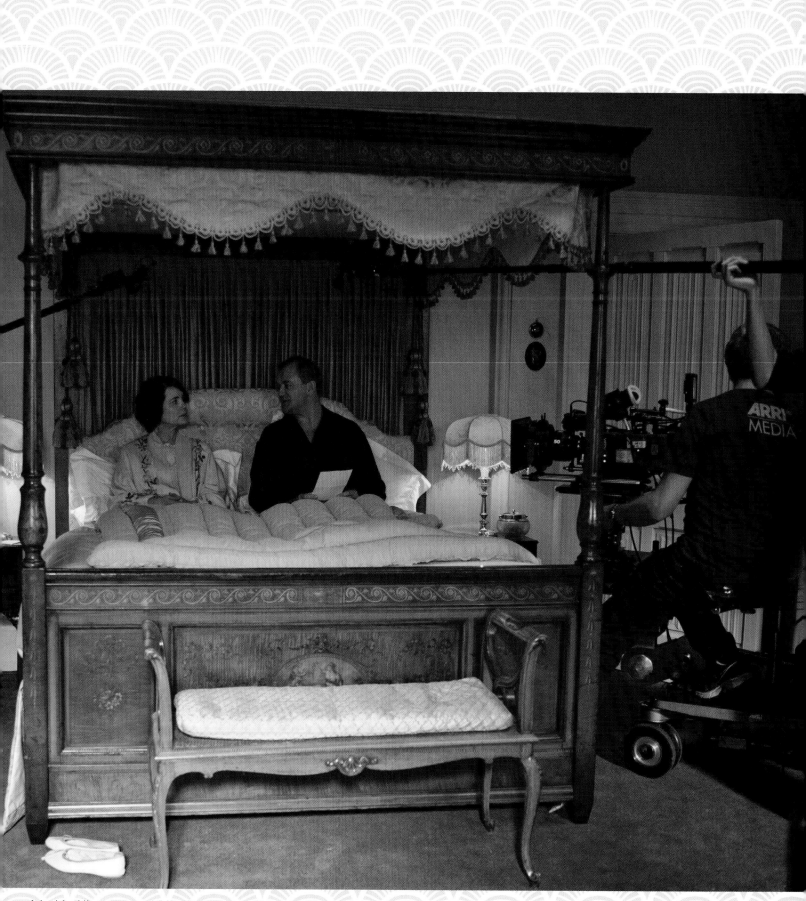

A behind-the-scenes shot of Robert and Cora, shocked when a letter brought by Mrs Hughes reveals O'Brien has left to work for Lady Flintshire.

But even after winning the fight, Robert stormed off to sleep in his dressing room, blaming Cora for Simon Bricker's flirtation. In a vast house, this small room is probably the place that affords Robert his greatest privacy. Yet, it is modest. He houses his small collection of snuff boxes here and photographs of Cora. There is a single bed, which is kept freshly made up but is rarely slept in. The bed is really for show, as we have seen Robert and Cora sleep together every night, but when they have had rows, as over Simon Bricker, or when Cora asked Robert to leave after the death of Sybil, for which she blamed him – then this small bed has proved very handy indeed.

The privacy has tempted Robert to stray, too. When feeling sidelined by the women of the house during the war, as they all busied themselves with the nursing and management of the convalescing officers, he found himself without any real purpose. Robert was too easily tempted by the warm shoulder of Jane, the housemaid. She seemed only too willing to listen and he sympathised with her own status as a war widow. Pulling her in to the dressing room, they shared a long kiss that might have led to a crumpling of his bed's sheets, had it not been for the approach of Bates, which brought Robert to his senses.

ROBERT

The thing is, I'm pretty sure she won't last 'til morning. And I don't want her to be frightened.

CORA

Then lay her here between us and she'll know she has someone who loves her very much next to her.

ROBERT

Two people who love her and each other, very much, on either side.

The room is a complete figment of the production designer Donal Woods's imagination, because there is, strangely, no dressing room by the bedroom used as Cora's at Highclere Castle. Donal's job was to create a room that would have fitted into the house but that also reflected Robert's character. The walls are painted in Farrow & Ball's London Clay, and almost all of the artefacts – even the precious snuff box collection – have been hired. 'It's a risk you take that things will be available when you need them again,' says Donal about the loaned items. 'Some things have changed because it's not sacrosanct – things get broken in real life, so it's fine.' For the final series, for the first time, the production was able to have Robert's dressing room actually leading directly off Cora's bedroom. For previous series, the production had had only one stage at Ealing Studios, but with two for the final series, they were able to build more sets and leave them up.

Robert's dressing room is also Bates's principal place of work – it is here that he will prepare and lay out his master's clothes, dress him, undress him, brush and hang the suits. Not all of Robert's clothes are kept here – things that aren't worn

often, such as travelling clothes, are kept in cedar-lined cupboards in the attic. But Robert's many official uniforms are kept here as well as his studs, cufflinks and plus fours. Hugh Bonneville's wardrobe consists of four country suits, one London suit, one white tie, one black tie (made in Savile Row), one set of morning tails and his army uniform. Everything is made by a tailor from Cosprop and Julian approves the fabrics – as he does for all the men's suits. There *are* slightly softer collars coming in but they're still pretty stiff.

Bates even cuts Robert's hair in here. Similarly, the male actors must have their hair cut every week so that the length is unchanged on the screen; as filming is rarely done in absolute chronological order. Nic Collins, hair and make-up designer, doesn't risk someone's hair looking short in the morning and long in the afternoon!

As any valet would, Bates spends much time in the dressing room alone. This gave Thomas and O'Brien an easy opportunity to set him up in the first series, when they took a snuff box and allowed the others to point the finger at Bates. Theft was the worst crime for a servant to be accused of – the fact that they were alone for periods of time in the house, amongst the priceless works of art, jewels and other valuables, meant that any employer had to trust them absolutely. A servant that stole was unemployable. Thomas and O'Brien, had they succeeded in their plot, would not only have cost Bates this job but any job in the future. Fortunately, they failed.

The intimacy of the room means this modest dressing room gives Bates a little privacy, too. It was in here that he was forced to confess to Mrs Hughes that he had put a contraption on his leg in his attempt to straighten out the limb, causing him agonising pain. So severe was the bleeding and the injury caused to his leg that Mrs Hughes, our stoic Scottish housekeeper, was brought to tears. She wasted no time in telling him to remove it and throw it in the river with a 'Good riddance!'

Cora also has a small sitting room upstairs, with a bureau for her own paperwork. She would most likely write and receive at least two or three letters daily. When her daughters were younger, keeping in regular touch with other mothers of a similar position would have been vital, to keep abreast of who the eligible young men were, who had become engaged and so on.

The sitting room is not filmed at Highclere but in the drawing room of West Wycombe Park, the location more usually used as the setting for Rosamund's London house. But we've only seen this room once, when Violet came to see Cora in the aftermath of the Kemal Pamuk disaster. Violet told Cora that she hoped she could have shown the same strength and that she did, after all, forgive Mary.

It was a lovely demonstration of how even the old-fashioned, upright Violet could get past anything if it meant protecting her kith and kin.

The Countess of Grantham
ELIZABETH McGOVERN

Cora was, in some ways, the genesis of *Downton Abbey*. The series came about when executive producer Gareth Neame and Julian had dinner together in London, in which they first mooted the idea of a television show set in a country house, following the lives of the characters above stairs and below, some time before the First World War. Although the two were excited at the time about the idea, Julian found himself a little unsure of revisiting the *Gosford Park* territory (the film he wrote for Robert Altman and which changed his life overnight when he won a Best Original Screenplay Oscar for it). But he went home and happened to pick up a book – *To Marry An English Lord* by Carol Wallace and Gail MacColl – about the Buccaneers. This was the nickname coined by novelist Edith Wharton for the American heiresses who came to Europe to marry into the aristocracy, earning themselves a title and

their husbands a fortune. Julian considered the fact that quite a lot is known about the more successful Buccaneers – the Duchess of Marlborough and Jennie Churchill (mother of Winston) for example – but what, he thought, of the more minor heiresses who handed over their money, married into an English family, leaving behind their own, as well as their friends and society, and found themselves some twenty years later living in a freezing cold castle in Yorkshire? So Cora was born, and a few days later Gareth received an email from Julian outlining all the rest of the characters and the plot of the first few episodes, including the heir drowning on the *Titanic* and the arrival of Matthew Crawley.

One of the key factors in Cora's existence that was played on a great deal at the beginning was that although it was her money that had enabled Downton Abbey to survive, her mother-in-law was not particularly grateful to her – Violet calls it 'a peculiar marriage'. When we first met Cora in 1912, she and Violet were at loggerheads over pretty much everything, a situation that had been sustained since 1890 when she and Robert had married. However, in their bid to smash the entail that prevented Mary inheriting the estate, Cora and Violet became allies and since then they have found a mutual respect and sympathy, if not quite unconditional love. 'They want the same things for the family,' said Elizabeth McGovern. 'I don't think they'll be soulmates but there's a shared devotion to their family and children and the well-being of the group.'

Cora has always been a dominated character – consider her mother, Martha Levinson, who took her daughter straight out of the schoolroom and into the ballrooms of London, eager to marry her off. When they see each other, said Elizabeth, 'The first ten minutes are euphoric and then things are just as complicated as they always were.' She has brought

Cora with a pregnant Sybil at the wedding of Mary and Matthew.

A countess would have an elegant dress for every occasion. Cora's dress was influenced by her fashionable young daughters.

offices overlooked. The walks of the family should not be open to view from the Servants' Departments and their sleeping quarters should be not only separate but separately approached.' The reasoning was that 'the family constitute one community: the servants another. Whatever may be their mutual regard and confidence as dwellers under the same roof, each class is entitled to shut its doors upon the other and be alone.'

The whole of the below stairs is one linked set at Ealing Studios, so that the movement between rooms is exactly as it appears on screen. By 1925 the number of servants has been reduced considerably but this has only added to the load of those that have remained behind as they struggle to maintain Carson's exacting Edwardian standards.

While the current bell board that dominates the servants' hall is a constant reminder that they are there to work, the contraption was actually once a symbol of freedom rather than servitude. Before the rigging up of all the rooms to the board

Handheld cameras are used to film the scenes in the servants' quarters, to emphasise their constant movement and work.

in the servants' hall, messages were passed around the house by the footmen. The footmen had, therefore, to sit at all times on hard wooden chairs within earshot of the family – usually in the hall (the one at Downton Abbey is perfectly suited to this as the hall sits in the middle of all the rooms making it very easy for the footman to hear anyone calling for him). They'd be called, given a message, and then have to find the maid or whomever, before returning to their chair. The board meant they were released from this arduous and dull task. All the servants would sit in their own hall where they could chat companionably, get on with any small task such as sewing or polishing, and if the bell went it would immediately be clear who was summoned and to where. By 1925, the bell board should really be electric – but, 'We kept the bells as they're more romantic,' says Donal Woods.

VIOLET

You're not in difficulties, are you?

ROBERT

No… But a butler, under butler, footmen, a valet, ladies' maids? To say nothing of the housemaids, the kitchen, the laundry, the gardens.

VIOLET

You think it's a bit too much in 1925?

Before the First World War, 1.4 million people worked as domestic servants. It was the largest single employment group – just outnumbering agricultural workers and coal miners – and was largely made up of women. Around 15 to 20 per cent of this number worked in houses of the nobility and landed gentry. But after the First World War these numbers were drastically reducing. Houses had learned to operate with fewer servants during the war and wage bills were on the increase (three times as much as before the war, says Robert at one point) thanks to new rules on pension contributions. Servants didn't want to return to their old jobs having had a taste of something else – service was becoming a less attractive option compared to jobs in the city with more free time to oneself. This left houses like Downton Abbey rather caught – on the one hand, they had to economise, recognising that the world was a different place and a dinner with six footmen could be seen as lavishly indulgent rather than fitting, but on the other their rooms were just as big and required just as much work to keep clean. And besides which – what was the point of a house like Downton if it wasn't to employ large numbers and entertain important guests? So began a new era in which the gentry had to find new roles for their estates, or sell up.

The key thing about the servants' hall is that it is very much their territory. The family rarely ventures downstairs and whenever they do it is with an apologetic air for intruding on their employees' privacy. Even Tom, who once belonged downstairs, finds it hard to go there without a very mixed response from the servants. When Cora came into the servants' hall to deliver a button that had fallen off her evening coat for

When there is a good cause, Mrs Hughes and Carson will allow the table to be pushed back so the servants can celebrate properly.

The family and servants celebrate the return of Mr and Mrs Carson from their honeymoon in Scarborough.

O'Brien to sew back on, the maid was affronted because Cora had heard her being uncomplimentary about Matthew Crawley. O'Brien felt that in the servants' hall she should be free to say whatever she liked without censorship. Cora, presumably, felt that as every brick in the place belonged to her husband, she had a right to expect loyalty expressed no matter where the servant happened to be standing.

Robert was seen below stairs on one important occasion – to announce the news that war was now at an end – but very little otherwise. Mary, too, has come through the green baize door only rarely – once to enquire whether anyone had posted a letter as an errand for Lavinia Swire when she was on her deathbed (the fortune of Downton Abbey hinged on the answer – thank goodness Daisy overheard the question).

Otherwise, the focus of the drama here has always been on the servants, whether it was William throwing a punch at Thomas, who had been making snide remarks to him for months, or the arrest of Bates for the murder of Vera. There were some fun sub-plots when O'Brien brought out the planchette (Ouija board), which was popular in the early 1920s. The piano in the corner has amused them once or twice, as when Daisy danced with Thomas, much to William's chagrin. There was the noisy card game of Racing Demon, led by visiting valet Mr Green, which failed to impress Carson. But above all, it is in this room that the servants' friendships, rivalries and romances are carried out, through meaningful glances across the table.

Any celebrations that the servants may have are enjoyed in here – their Christmas lunch, the one time of year they do not have to serve a meal to the family, being the longest and most enjoyable, complete with paper hats. Nor do they have to attend to the family drinks at midnight on New Year's Eve, so that they may have a party of their own. But the most charming was the return of Mr and Mrs Carson from their honeymoon, when paper chains and hearts were pinned up around the room, punch was served and a delicious spread of cheeses and jam tarts was laid on.

'I try to think of reasons for the upstairs to go downstairs,' says Julian. 'Some are quite simple – Cora needs to talk about the menu, or Mary and Robert might be worried about Carson. But you can't do that too often and sometimes it needs something extraordinary like Carson getting married. It's completely realistic to show the family attending the wedding – it would have been considered rather ill bred not to have done it.'

CARSON

Well now m'lord. This is the thing. Won't it be confusing if we're to be called Mr Carson and Mrs Carson? Rather as we resisted Anna's being Mrs Bates? Would you think it very irregular if we continued being known as Carson and Mrs Hughes?

ROBERT

Hallelujah. You have made me a happy man.

Mr Molesley

KEVIN DOYLE

The tragicomic sight of Molesley in the servants' hall never fails to rouse a smile. The character was originally devised by Julian as little more than a narrative means to an end; a way of showing how even an established professional such as Matthew would be unused to this new life he was going to inherit. In their early scenes, when Molesley is frustrated by Matthew's reluctance to employ his valeting skills, Julian found that he was so moved by Kevin Doyle's touching and funny performance that he was reluctant to write him out. Hence Molesley's rather rocky career path from butler to valet to footman under the employ of the Crawley family.

Strictly speaking, Molesley ought to have been referred to by his first name as footman but everyone agreed it would be too hard to get used to. By and large it seems to be the case at Downton Abbey that changing a name for reasons of promotion is fine – for example, from Thomas to Mr Barrow – but to take someone backwards seems rather to rub salt in the wound. There's a certain fudging of the rules at Downton – Anna should be Bates but that would be too confusing with her husband as Bates, too; and Mrs Hughes should be Mrs Carson but no one, even the happy couple themselves, could quite get their heads round it. (Also, the 'Mrs' before she was married was

Even at a wedding with Baxter, optimism does not come easily to Molesley.

Molesley is increasingly seen in civvies as he looks beyond the boundaries of Downton Abbey.

MOLESLEY

I believe that education is the gate that leads to any future worth having.

simply a mark of respect for an older woman, as it is for Mrs Patmore.) Houses and their families had their own ways of doing things in so many matters. There's the true story of the parlourmaid who was told on starting her job that she would henceforth be known as Mary, because the mistress liked her parlourmaids to be called Mary.

Molesley was born and brought up in Downton village – we first met his widowed father, Bill, in series one as the gardener of beautiful roses who finally wins the prize in the flower show after Violet gives in to Isobel's campaign. Julian describes his character as 'the downstairs Edith', the man who somehow always just misses the train. He's certainly had his share of disappointments: he liked Anna but she was in love with Bates; the night he thought he might start work as a valet for Robert, Bates suddenly returned; he narrowly avoided being conscripted for the war when Violet declared he had trouble with his lungs – Dr Clarkson suspected this may not be true but decided not to pursue the issue; when Matthew was killed he lost his job and was forced to work as a delivery boy and road mender. When eventually he returned to Downton Abbey it was as footman – a considerable downgrade and something that was driven home by Carson pointedly reminding him to wear white gloves to serve the dinner. Even his more minor attempts to improve his life seem bound to fail – as when he dyed his hair black to appear younger. By series six, things seem to be on the turn. In Baxter, he finds a sympathetic ear, one who even seems to like him and in turn, she boosts his confidence.

In the final series, Molesley realises that there may no longer be an opportunity for him to work as butler in the future, at Downton or anywhere, so he starts to explore alternatives.

> DAISY
>
> *Is that the end of service for you?*
>
> MOLESLEY
>
> *Service is ending for most of us, Daisy. I've just got a head start.*

Kevin admits that he is not too distant from Molesley: 'I'm quite reluctant to come forward in most things – I do have this ridiculous respect for authority and status, despite trying otherwise (I always defer to a uniform). Had I lived in such times, I imagine I would have had quite a similar, modest career path. Molesley and I walk hand-in-hand!' Although I would have to contest that – Kevin has a much better sense of humour and is rather more self-deprecating than his footman alias.

Kevin feels sympathy for the real people of the era, having learned how restricted their lives were in terms of opportunities: 'Not just the servants, who could only look forward for the most part to a life of service, but also the women led remarkably limited lives. It seemed to be all about marriage and children and it was lovely to see Lady Edith breaking through those restrictions and expectations.' (Note how a below stairs actor calls a member of the family by their title and name! Or perhaps that's just Kevin's natural sense of deference again.)

Downton has provided some happy moments – not least in his own character arc and even storylines. 'There was a scene when Mrs Hughes and Molesley were talking of Jesus and Mary Magdalene and she mentioned that Jesus ate with Mary. Molesley replies: "Ah, we can't be sure that he ate with her – he *did* allow her to wash his feet." I loved that line, the certainty with which he said it.' Off set, Kevin does his best to avoid the *Downton* hullabaloo – 'you want to keep it as fresh as series one' – but did enjoy one particularly nice glass of wine: 'I was in a restaurant in LA, sat by myself reading a book, having my meal and the owner came over and mentioned that some people over at the other side of the room would like to buy me a glass of wine. I thought, "This is straight from a movie." Nicest glass of wine I ever had.'

Footmen had liveried uniforms that were made on Savile Row
– for the modern man they are stiff and uncomfortable.

Andy

MICHAEL FOX

We first met Andy Parker in London, where he was hired as temporary footman during the celebrations for the wedding of Rose and Atticus. After Jimmy was summarily sacked and Molesley was worn out by doing all the footmen's jobs alone, he was brought back when Carson took shameless advantage of Robert's windfall when the della Francesca painting was sold.

Similarly, Michael Fox didn't know his would turn out to be a permanent part in the show: 'When I had my audition it was murmured it would continue but it was a big maybe. Luckily for me, it did. I was quite happy – I would have taken one episode!' Michael feels quite at ease in his livery, too. 'I always wanted to do period drama,' he says. 'I like the formality of it.'

Nevertheless, he's had to get used to the upright bearing of a good footman: 'My lower back was aching a lot the first couple of weeks because of having to straighten myself and put my shoulders back. Because I'm taller, I do hunch slightly, but Alastair (Bruce the on-set historical advisor) pays great attention to the detail of posture.'

Andy has turned out to be less of a city boy than he thought himself to be. Despite having grown up in London, it is in Yorkshire that he finds his true metier, and is a willing hand for Mr Mason and his pigs. 'He's not as secure in the house as Carson would have been,' says Michael. 'He's not wanting to live his whole life there. What education he can muster to pull together, to try and better himself, he tries. Straight from the off he thinks he's vulnerable, so he has to think about what interests him and he comes across farming. This is what he really loves.'

Although a city boy by background, Andy finds he is most comfortable at Mr Mason's farm.

Andy ready for dinner – a footman's clothes changed little during the period.

ANDY

*Not everyone's right
for what they're born to.*

The household is managed from Mrs Hughes's desk.

MRS HUGHES'S SITTING ROOM

Carson knocks at the door and brings in a decanter and two glasses.

One couldn't say of Carson or Mrs Hughes that they are the type to let it all hang out – but if they come close to doing so, it's in the housekeeper's sitting room at Downton Abbey. Phyllis Logan and Jim Carter have always enjoyed filming the scenes in either here or the butler's pantry as a chance for the actors to reveal something of their characters' real selves beneath their strict professionalism. 'Right at the beginning when Alastair [Bruce] was giving us the instructions, he told us the sitting room and pantry were the only places where they weren't on show and weren't heads of department, so they could just be themselves,' says Phyllis. 'And there's always more dialogue between us in those scenes – we can get stuck in.'

The set for Mrs Hughes's sitting room has also developed over the years: 'It's grown bigger,' says Donal Woods, 'it's one of the best-dressed rooms now with the most personal effects.' Mrs Hughes was, until her marriage, in the classic servant's position of being the very best housekeeper without ever having actually run a house of her own. In the sitting room, occupied by her for at least fifteen years, she has been able to furnish and dress it to the very best of her standards as well as to her own feminine desires. It is singular in the servants' quarters for containing any personal touches at all – Carson's pantry is only functional and the bedrooms contain very few belongings that are not for practical purposes. But Mrs Hughes has her desk, cluttered with paperwork, a small posy of flowers and a light with a pretty glass shade. There's a few books on a shelf, a rug on the floor, a favoured cushion on the chair. Not to mention the famous toaster that, much to Carson's alarm, burned the bread when it was first used.

Mrs Hughes lets her guard down in here not only to Mr Carson but also to her friend and ally, Mrs Patmore. Their relationship has developed over the years. 'They are women of similar age and background in service,' says Phyllis. 'It makes sense for them to get on rather than not. They do rely on one another.'

As the first series began, they were coming to the end of a long battle over the store cupboard, but this was nothing unusual. The thinking behind the arrangement of houses like Downton was that the housekeeper was in charge of the ordering and accounts for the stores, so it made better sense for her to keep note of what was used. But it always infuriated the cooks.

The turning point came when Mrs Hughes had her breast cancer scare; it was Mrs Patmore, as her only fellow woman of similar age below stairs, that she turned to. In the end, she was given the all-clear but it brought the two of them closer. They certainly recognised that they were stronger as allies. 'The dynamic changed between her and Mrs Patmore – things had been fractious until then,' says Phyllis. 'It was a great storyline, an interesting one to do. I'm glad she survived!' Since then we've seen them enjoy a few moments together – not least when Mrs Hughes summoned up the courage to tell Mrs Patmore that she saw Joe Tufton flirting with several young ladies at the fair, much to the cook's giggling relief!

In series six, Mrs Hughes confided in her friend that she was worried about the intimate side of married life with Mr Carson – entirely understandable given that she was a woman who had never before been to bed with a man. But as Mrs Patmore hadn't either, she was rather in the dark as to how to deal with it.

Mrs Hughes's sitting room gives her the privacy to discuss matters that she wouldn't want overheard.

But the housekeeper's sitting room was not devised as a place for her pleasure. It was principally an office, a place of work. From here the housekeeper would draw up her rotas for the housemaids, her lists and budget for the stores and make careful notes in her diary of guests coming to stay. With a big set of keys jangling at her waist, Mrs Hughes would also check on the linens (from bedsheets to napkins) which would need careful rotating to prevent overuse of any one set, as well as the china – as when Mrs Hughes suggested changing the Meissen for the Spode set. Housekeepers were also responsible for any mending of linens that might need to be done. Knowing such detail gave them power over their mistresses, should they wish to wield it. The Viscountess Hambleden recalled that on her marriage, the housekeeper resented her 'to such an extent that she became extremely clever at making me look rather idiotic, like giving my grandest guests cotton sheets, unbeknownst to me, when we had linen ones'.

In her sitting room Mrs Hughes has the privacy to admonish any housemaids if necessary – she's certainly had her troubles with the ambitious, amorous, Ethel (who had a baby by Major Bryant) and Edna (who set her sights at Tom) in the past.

Perhaps the cosy nature of this room lends itself well to being a place of confession too. In here, Tom admitted that he had slept with Edna – an act that he knew would lead to her dismissal. More distressingly, it was here that Anna, crying and badly shaken, told her that she had been attacked and raped by Mr Green. Later, Bates came in to Mrs Hughes's room to extract the truth from her as to what had happened to his wife – he succeeded, and she was chilled by his response.

The camera captures Mr Carson and Mrs Hughes in a moment of intense conversation, but note how even alone they do not touch each other.

Mrs Hughes allows Daisy to use her sitting room for her lessons with Miss Bunting.

On rare occasions, others have been lent the room for their own privacy, too. Fortunately, only Mrs Hughes knows there's a grating in the wall that means any conversation in here can be eavesdropped on – something that she found came in handy when Vera Bates arrived to threaten her husband. Mrs Hughes offered the room for them to talk in – and through the grating she heard Vera telling Bates she will go to the papers with the story about the Turk dying in Lady Mary's bed, and that Anna will feature in the story as the woman who helped to move the corpse.

For the most part, it has always seemed that Mrs Hughes was content with her lot. It was revealed early on that she had once had the chance to marry but chose not to be a farmer's wife. In the context of the times, Mrs Hughes was a career woman and a successful one at that – to be the housekeeper of an earl's household was a pinnacle to be proud of. Unlike Carson, Mrs Hughes does not define herself by her job but she is nonetheless proud of her standards and a professional in meeting them. But as she grew older it started to prey on her mind that retirement may not offer her relief from work. Mrs Hughes faced either working until she dropped, or the workhouse if her employers did not look after her (and one couldn't guarantee something that was not, in the end, a statutory obligation).

After Carson's suggestion that they buy a house together, Mrs Hughes pretended to go along with his plans but when he found a property, she was forced to admit she had no money left and was not in a position to share the investment – any spare income over the years had been spent on paying for an ill sister. Fortunately, it turned out that Carson had only been using the house as an excuse to share his life with Mrs Hughes. The conversation took place in her sitting room one night and led to Carson's proposal… and Mrs Hughes's delighted, immediate, acceptance.

Luckily for Mrs Hughes, Carson adores her and offered a much more tempting alternative. But if they hadn't married – what might she have had to look forward to? At the start of the 1920s, the pensionable population was largely vulnerable, infirm and in dire financial states. Without savings, Carson, Mrs Hughes and Mrs Patmore would have been eligible to receive ten shillings a week, once they were seventy years old. But this barely covered the most basic standard of living. In 1925, a new contributory pension was introduced, which was part-financed by employers and employees. However, many failed to qualify if they hadn't made the contributions – this may have been Mrs Hughes's position, given that all her money had gone to her sister's care. In short, she would have been out on her ear.

MRS HUGHES
You're such an old curmudgeon.

CARSON
Don't say you're going off me.

MRS HUGHES
No, because you're my curmudgeon and that makes all the difference.

A glass of port at the end of the night does little to reassure Mrs Hughes that marriage to Mr Carson will spell the end of her worries.

Mrs Hughes

PHYLLIS LOGAN

Julian Fellowes describes Mrs Hughes as 'a reasonably just person because she is not tremendously on anyone's side'. In her thirty years of service, she has learned that there are always two sides to every story and it's probably just as well not to land too heavily on either one (she's even been known to help Thomas out). Without being enthralled by the family she works for, she is more dependable as the 'intelligent, moral leader of below stairs' as her creator says of her. Phyllis Logan is perhaps a tiny bit more forgiving: 'She can be a bit of a "nippy sweetie" (irritable, sharp-tongued person) as we say in Scotland. She can take people down when she feels like it,' she laughs. 'I'm not nearly as nippy sweet as she can be –

she's got a barb to her. I might be like that very, very rarely. I'd like to think I've got a kind heart – and I think she has, too. But where she doesn't care what people think about her, I probably do. She's a foil to Carson – her Scottishness is more prone to socialism and that's my background also – we're similar in that respect. And we both have a sense of humour.' But Phyllis doesn't share her character's professional skills: 'She's very organised and that's not me at all. I dither about and it takes me forever to do anything!'

I'd heard a rumour that Phyllis was the only actress on the show still wearing a corset. 'Absolutely true!' she says. 'She's still back in the Edwardian period. I don't mind – it makes you look and stand differently.' Having

Mrs Hughes with her stalwart ally, Mrs Patmore. They have had long years in service together.

Plain day dresses for the servants are given texture to add depth and interest on screen.

MRS HUGHES

If you want me you can have me, to quote Oliver Cromwell, warts and all.

been on the show since it began, Phyllis is good friends with the rest of the cast: 'All the below stairs get on great because we do a lot together. Jim and I will often sit and natter and have a chinwag in the dressing room. We often get the cars in and out with Lesley and Sophie (McShera), too.' While Phyllis's own work at Downton Abbey is enjoyable, she's witnessed the contrast to the lot of the servants they portray. 'You see that even when the family go away, they're still running the fort and she gets everyone spring cleaning. There was never any respite.'

Unlike most of the audience, Phyllis was a little uncertain when it came to Mrs Hughes and Carson getting married. 'Jim thought they should but I thought it might change the dynamic,' she says. 'Jim's idea was that it was what the public demanded and in the end that was what was so nice about it. Their late love came to the fore. They have had their ups and downs but always had a little thing for each other. It came down to the fact they had great respect and fondness.'

With Mrs Hughes's future settled, Phyllis's still holds unknown excitements, 'There's a slight element of trepidation,' she confesses. Whatever happens next – and we can be sure it will be good – Phyllis has thoroughly enjoyed her years at Downton. 'There's no challenge. Getting up in the morning at five o'clock or whatever – it's just a joy. Every second.'

Mrs Hughes is the keeper of the keys.

Mr and Mrs Carson – as they are never called.

Carson is interrupted from his work.

CARSON'S PANTRY

INT. CARSON'S PANTRY. DAY.

Carson is decanting port. He has stretched gauze across a silver funnel and now lights a candle to place behind the flow of wine as he pours. Mrs Hughes is watching him.

Carson may be the most senior of all the servants, the longest serving at Downton Abbey (he arrived as a young footman in the days of the former Lord Grantham) and the man in charge of not only everything below stairs but also above stairs in almost equal measure. Any sensible master soon learns to bow to his butler's demands if he wants a comfortable house. Yet, Carson's private quarters are hardly luxurious and are not even particularly designed for his pleasure. The butler is given the pantry only because he is the one deemed the most trustworthy: his room is essentially the safe for the family silver. (In real life, the silver we see occasionally when the safe door is opened is largely plastic.) In some households, the butler used to sleep in the pantry to safeguard the valuables. Fortunately, this isn't expected of Carson.

Not that Carson would mind too much. He knows his pantry is a very important room and as it is wholly designed for the purpose of him carrying out his work, it suits him very well indeed. If one thinks of the below stairs quarters as the backstage of a theatre – a metaphor that is entirely appropriate as the work that the servants do above stairs is as much about putting on a show as anything else – then the butler's pantry is the store for the more expensive props. Carson will count and check the silver regularly, polishing the more fragile pieces himself, ensuring that any marks or scratches are attended to professionally.

In this room, he'll also carefully decant the port (filtering it through a muslin cloth to catch the dregs). Of course, there's important servant management to attend to – a ledger in which the wages are recorded, a book in which to make notes on the wines. Managing the cellar is one of the butler's most significant duties and Lord Grantham depends on Carson's many years of experience to choose the best wines to accompany Mrs Patmore's food, to spend the household budget on building the cellar as wisely as possible and to taste the wine before dinner in case it is corked. He must also know when to open the wines, the correct temperature at which to store them and, of course, when to pour the wine at dinner. When one considers that today a sommelier at a grand hotel will train for at least three years, one understands better that a butler's work was one of skill and nuanced taste.

Keeping a tally on the wine's stock was perhaps necessary when it came to the less scrupulous of the servants. Thomas, in the first series, was almost badly caught out – he tried to point the finger at Bates and got O'Brien and Daisy to do so too, but Bates reminded them that he hadn't so much as sipped a drop of alcohol since arriving at Downton Abbey. (We learned later that he had had an ugly history as a drunk after the Boer War.) Bates, to his credit, refused to implicate Thomas in return, knowing that an accusation of theft is something a servant can almost never recover from. Though it's far from certain that he hasn't regretted that moment of nobility since.

Other tasks are completed in here, such as ironing the newspapers in the morning (to dry the ink, as O'Brien told Daisy in the first episode). The pantry is also where Carson may talk to any of the other servants privately, as when he was forced to ask Bates if he had stolen the wine from the cellar. Later, poor Daisy admitted she had lied about it – there is little that would have been more frightening for a young kitchen maid like her than to stand in front of the butler's desk and confess to a fib. Later, when Carson severely admonished Daisy for speaking out to the family she was visibly less afraid as she had not only grown up, she knew life in 1925 had more to offer her than work as a servant.

It was also in the butler's pantry that Jimmy insisted Thomas be given a bad reference after he had entered his room one night and tried to kiss him. And this room was where Carson offered Molesley work as a footman – a sad step down for the former butler and valet – and was rebuffed, much to his shock. (You can't keep a man like Molesley up for long, though – he soon came back and asked for the job.)

Most embarrassingly, for Mrs Patmore at least, this was where she tried to find out, on behalf of Mrs Hughes, in advance of the wedding, if Carson expected her to perform full wifely duties. It took some while before they were both able to reach the point, although Carson was surprisingly candid, if loving.

While Carson does his best to hold the modern world at bay, he can't prevent it from infiltrating his room entirely. A telephone was installed in series two, and it was not an instrument that Carson welcomed. The other servants had a giggle when they caught him practising his 'telephone voice' on it. But pity the poor man. As a young adult in the Victorian era, the fastest form of communication was a messenger on horseback. These things take adjusting to.

Of course, there have to be perks and, now and again, Carson allows himself a little treat. When a bottle hasn't been finished and Lord Grantham has gone away, then Carson will permit a glass for him and Mrs Hughes at the end of the night. It's in this

Sergeant Willis and Mr Carson have a cup of tea together but the atmosphere is not light – this was when Bates was interviewed over the death of Mr Green. The crew must huddle in the small room for filming.

Carson and Mrs Hughes can discuss the servants in private – in this case Thomas and Jimmy.

room, as well as Mrs Hughes's sitting room, that Julian has slowly laid the path for the two of them. He says he always knew he wanted them to end up together, but he wanted the viewer to realise they were well suited almost before they did. In the very first episode, Carson explained that he was worried about the family and their troubles over the inheritance, and Mrs Hughes admonished him. 'They're all the family I've got,' was Carson's explanation. She asked him, then, if he had ever wished that he'd gone another way – worked in a shop or factory, had a wife and children, admitting that she thought about it sometimes. So we have watched the two of them have a little chat now and then; as the two most senior servants and as the parent figures of the others below stairs they are able to talk freely about their concerns. Carson and Mrs Hughes relax as best as they know how when they are with each other.

We got our romantic episode in this room when Mrs Hughes came at last to realise that Carson wanted a proper marriage with her, not a 'warm companionship'. After reassuring her that she would not disappoint him, Carson did what we had all longed for him to do but perhaps never expected to see: he took Mrs Hughes's face in his hands, looked into her eyes and kissed her.

CARSON

Hard work and diligence weigh more than beauty in the real world.

Carson is in charge of the cellar.

Mr Carson

JIM CARTER

The upright Mr Carson, long-standing servant to Downton Abbey – he arrived as footman when Violet and the former Lord Grantham were in situ – is played by the genial and gentle actor Jim Carter. He brings warmth to Carson, where he might have been too rigid and too unforgiving. Carson may worry about things that seem irrelevant to the modern audience – the pudding glasses, the right kind of spoons – but we never laugh at him. Instead, we understand his desire to get things right and his bewilderment at a changing world that has less and less use for him as time goes on.

In giving Carson a back story early on that was at odds with his role as butler – when it was revealed that he had been on the music hall stage – Julian conferred even more humanity on the character.

Jim sympathises with Carson: 'Like him, I'm a fan of manners and politeness. Usually. And I'm punctual in the extreme,' he says. But, other than their eyebrows, he laughs, the similarities end there. 'I find routine irksome and boring and I only dress formally under duress.' This explains Julian's consciousness of Jim's displeasure at the dining room scenes. Jim's least favourite line is: '"Dinner is

With Lady Mary, Carson can often be found to be a little more off-guard, as here with the new gramophone.

Carson's demeanour changes little even when he is not at work.

served, m'lady" as it involves me waiting behind a door for most of the day.' But Jim knows his craft and although he is a popular man on set, he's got a particular ally, which he shares with Hugh Bonneville: 'Every actor's best friend on set is the lighting cameraman.'

Carson's most important relationship is, of course, with Robert, who he respects as an earl and his master, although their partnership is more nuanced than that – they have a shared responsibility to run the house. But his heart is ruled by two women – Mary and Mrs Hughes. Jim particularly enjoyed 'the slow-burn wooing of Mrs Hughes' as it developed over several years.

A lifelong fan of cricket – Jim ran his own club in London for many years – filming the cricket episode was his favourite week of all. The cricket outfit is quickly cited as his favourite costume – not that Carson has too many to wear. The joke is always that Jim has had the least fittings of anyone on the show – after the first one for the first series, Carson has never changed his costume. The fame that Downton brought has given Jim some 'lovely invitations – to the President of the MCC's box at Lords, the White House and the Chelsea Flower Show. But most of all, it's given me the chance to help so many worthwhile causes with fundraising and publicity.'

Mrs Hughes and Carson have a day out at the Fat Stock Show.

A married man, Carson looks contented despite the formality of the white tie that he wears to serve dinner.

CARSON

*I've never been called a
liberal in my life and I
don't intend to start now.*

Mrs Patmore presides over her realm and all who serve within it.

THE KITCHEN

MRS PATMORE: *Daisy? What's happened to you?*
I said you could go for a drink of water,
not a trip up the Nile.

The kitchen of a great country house could be a hellish place – hot, stocked with knives, the air full of temper. It was a world within a world – the cook's own domain, with its own retinue of servants and its own rules. The cook and her maids ate separately, worked apart from the rest of the servants and almost never had anything to do directly with the family. Yet it was their work that kept the house spinning on its axis. Delicious food was delivered above stairs to the state rooms at least four times a day, as well as to the rest of the household, sitting down to eat in the servants' hall. With few kitchen gadgets and almost none of today's advantages – no freezer, no ready-made meals – to produce ambitious dishes, the pressure on the cook and her staff was immense.

Any good employer knew that well-fed servants would be happy servants and if important guests were also impressed with the excellent quality of the food, they were likely to want to come and stay again. In short, good food was the key to a well-run, successful household. It did mean, however, that the fortunes – never mind the stomachs – of the household were more or less dependent on the cook and her maids and that was a lot of responsibility to bear.

And yet, despite the pressure, the kitchen has been the hub of many intrigues. Around the huge wooden table, as Mrs Patmore rolls pastry or Daisy slices lemons, we've seen a fair share of Downton drama.

Right in the first episode, Daisy realised only just in time that she had sent up a bowl of salt of sorrel (used for cleaning brass) to sprinkle on a dish of chicken. Reprieved at the last second from poisoning the entire family, Daisy vowed to be good, always. Alfred, the footman, learned how to advance his cooking well enough to get himself a position in the kitchens of the Ritz. And if the occasion warrants it, Mrs Patmore has been known to open a bottle of wine in the kitchen to celebrate.

The desk where Mrs Patmore works out her menus is within the kitchen itself.

The romance that has taken place in this room has been a little one-sided, perhaps. When William proposed to Daisy, it was an affecting scene: in his uniform, about to go to war, Daisy gave William a photograph of herself. She'd had to go to the village to have it taken especially; soldiers, for obvious reasons, took comfort in having a picture of their sweethearts with them at the front. William, happy that she has given it to him, proposed as best as his shy manner would allow: 'You know what I'm going to ask you... So, will you?' Daisy tried to put him off, telling him he couldn't possibly be sure, before Mrs Patmore intervened and accepted on her behalf, telling him it was just what Daisy wanted. They embraced but while William's eyes were closed, Daisy stared at Mrs Patmore.

The development of the relationship between Mrs Patmore and Daisy has been one of the nicest things to watch. When Daisy worked as a kitchen maid in the first few years, Mrs Patmore was very tough on her but she couldn't afford a single mistake. One slip up and the soufflés would be sunk, along with Mrs Patmore's reputation.

As the series have gone on, Mrs Patmore has become a little better humoured, which could be down to the fact that Daisy is now the under cook and able to help shoulder the heavy workload. Their relationship has also developed into one of true friendship and mutual respect, which makes for a nicer working atmosphere.

As friends, they have confided in each other – whether it was Daisy's broken heart, her regret over the 'lie' to William, her plans to do exams, or Mrs Patmore's grief over her nephew Archie. She's even admitted to Daisy that she 'might be' a bit jealous of Mrs Hughes's marriage. In fact, they became so close that when it looked as if Mrs Patmore might become friends with Daisy's father-in-law Mr Mason, Daisy felt threatened – if they had each other, she might be left with no one at all, again.

Newfangled kitchen gadgets have slowly arrived, although they have not been welcomed with open arms by Mrs Patmore, who is afraid of being replaced by an electric beater if not by 'a woman in the village' (she gets mentioned as a threatening possibility now and then), but they must nevertheless have taken some of the strain off the work.

An exciting new addition to the kitchen in the sixth series was the arrival of the refrigerator, a Frigidaire. An original 1920s artefact, it has been repainted by the props department to make it look new as it would have been to Mrs Patmore. It's chunky, like a modern Smeg, and with just a couple of shelves inside – far smaller than the modern fridge used to keep food for a family, let alone a household of some twenty-odd people. But it was thrilling for Downton – enough to bring Cora and Robert down to the kitchens late one night, when Robert did what all of us must have done when looking inside a fridge just before bed: reach inside for a chicken leg to munch on.

As the series have progressed the relationship between Daisy and Mrs Patmore has grown to one of perfectly co-ordinated professionalism and friendship.

Despite the onward march of progress in the world outside, the installation of electric lighting below stairs in the second series is the only really serious change the kitchen has undergone since 1912. The paintwork hasn't changed colour, the large black range is still the principal oven and the huge wooden table – built on set as the original hired table was too heavy to shift at the beginning and end of filming – is the same. While the details around the kitchen are absolutely spot on – the Household Monitor, the small desk on which Mrs Patmore sits and works out her menus, the copper saucepans hanging on the wall – there's just one thing that isn't, perhaps, exactly right for the period and that is that all the kitchen's action takes place in the one room.

A large house such as Downton Abbey would be more likely to have had a number of rooms for food preparation, including a still room (originally the 'distillery room') with its own maid, who would have got the breakfast trays ready as well as make the jams, jellies and pastries. There might have also been a vegetable maid, who would do nothing but scrub, peel and chop in a side room, and a scullery maid who would wash up in an ante-room, as well as lay the fires upstairs and black-lead the stove. Instead, the decision was taken that the show had reached its limit on characters, so these last maids were amalgamated into one kitchen maid – Daisy – giving her rather an onerous workload.

Kitchen maids did exist, of course, and were generally the ones left with all the jobs that no one else wanted to do – they were the lowest of the low in the servant hierarchy. Margaret Powell, who began her career in that position, recalled in her memoir, *Below Stairs*, that when she joined her first household no one even knew who she was: 'No one bothers to introduce a kitchen maid. You're just looked at as if you're something the cat brought in.'

After the war, when Daisy had been promoted to under cook, she grumbled for some while about the lack of a kitchen maid. So it was hard for her to say anything when Mrs Patmore introduced the pretty Ivy, even if it did happen just as she was about to admit to Alfred that she was sweet on him. Thereafter, much to Mrs Patmore's despair, there was an ongoing romantic tangle that looked impossible to resolve: Daisy liked Alfred, Alfred liked Ivy, Ivy liked Jimmy. Not that Jimmy minded the attention too much and was quite happy to court the kitchen maid, thinking there would be a bit of slap and tickle in it for him at least. He danced with her in the kitchen, much to her delight. After Ivy left, she was not replaced, of course, so the kitchen struggles on in the sixth series without that extra pair of hands.

Julian and the other producers also took the view that it would be dramatically more interesting to have all the work – and, therefore, the conversations – going on around the one table, which is why we see Mrs Patmore garnish the consommé at the same time as Daisy beats the eggs for a mousse and the footmen collect the dishes.

The kitchen is a place of intrigue, scheming and romance in amongst the hot pans and sizzling dishes: Daisy and Ivy; Jimmy and Ivy; Daisy and Alfred.

MRS PATMORE

Daisy mustn't find out I don't know how to work it.

MRS HUGHES

Why ever not?

MRS PATMORE

Because it makes her part of the future and leaves me stuck in the past. Don't you see?

Sophie McShera snatches a moment with her very twenty-first-century mobile phone between takes on set and (inset) filming with a more appropriate gadget.

You have a talent that none of the rest of us have. Just find out what it is, and use it. It's doing nothing that's the enemy.

Mrs Patmore and Daisy teach Sybil to cook.

One key factor in the life of a cook was that of all the senior servants she had the least interaction with the family above stairs. No uniform is worn – though we rarely see a kitchen maid out of her cap and plain, clean apron over a printed dress – and with the kitchen out of the general remit of anyone else, the cook was queen of her own realm. Once a week, she would meet with the mistress of the house to discuss the menus for the family, servants and nursery but otherwise, that was it.

The kitchen was kept spotless – the range would be black-leaded daily, the brass knobs shining, the pans scrubbed as soon as they were used – and with food carried up the stairs by the footmen several times a day, there was certainly no room to hide. But the bottom line was that Mrs Patmore was her own boss. There was little need on her part for the constant deference the other servants had to show the family with their 'yes, m'lady' and 'yes, m'lord', their on-call responses to the bell board and the uniforms that were the marker of their place in the house. Even when Lady Sybil came to the kitchen in the second series, to learn some basics in cooking before leaving to train as a nurse in York, Mrs Patmore found it hard to remember how she ought to talk to any member of the family and soon found herself passing comment as she would with any maid's first attempt to make a cake – bluntly, in short.

As Mrs Patmore grew older, like Mrs Hughes, it could have been a concern as to how she would manage a life in retirement. So it certainly must have been a lifesaver when her aunt died and left her enough money to buy herself a small cottage. Although Mrs Patmore could probably have relied on the kindness of her employers to look after her in her dotage, there was no obligation on their part to do so and should they lose the estate – it's not as if they haven't been close to it in the past – there would have been nothing for her at all.

Mrs Patmore and Cora discuss the menus each week.

One lovely development in the kitchen in the sixth series is the appearance of the children, George, Sybbie and Marigold, below stairs. It was very usual for the children to befriend the servants, finding them on the whole sympathetic to their childish demands and enjoying perhaps a moment or two to play with them as respite from work. I particularly liked the scene in the sixth series, when George and Marigold sat on the table as Mrs Patmore poured cake mix into the tins. George made the time-honoured request of children all over the world: 'Can I lick the bowl?'

At Ealing Studios, watching a scene from episode five of the sixth series being filmed in the kitchen, one notices the splashes of colour on the table – a colander of green leaves, a heap of peeled orange carrots – all carefully thought through by Lisa Heathcote, the food stylist. Daisy chops fresh herbs with a knife, until the decision is made to change to a mezzaluna. A tray of tasty-looking roast potatoes – in reality, stone cold and not that nice to eat – is put beside her. Although in the scene only a few lines are said – the take lasts thirty seconds, if that – there's a constant motion of activity the entire time. In between takes, make-up is touched up and the actors slip back into the conversation they were having. It feels relaxed and yet everyone knows exactly what they're expected to do, where they need to stand, all directed by Michael Engler, who is responsible for this particular episode. One sees the silent kitchen maids repeatedly walk in the same place, Sophie McShera perfectly repeats the action each time, Jim Carter says his line as freshly on the fourth take as on the first – it's a display of utter professionalism. Exactly, in short, as the kitchen staff would behave.

Mrs Patmore

LESLEY NICOL

Ask Lesley Nicol in what ways she is most like her character and she can't help herself, even after all these years: 'Well, I'm a great cook...' she begins and then bursts out laughing. The irony of the show is that Lesley's character is known the world over for being an expert cook but in real life, she can just about open a tin of soup. In all ways, fond as she is of Mrs Patmore, Lesley finds she has little in common with her character, 'We live in different worlds. It would be hard to find similarities,' she explains. She's enjoyed, however, the way in which she has grown to know the cook: 'You pare them back, and the layers are allowed better to show.'

Mrs Patmore has been working at Downton Abbey for a long time and as a senior servant who is excellent at her job she is highly prized. Good cooks were tightly held on to by their employers, which is why it is no surprise that Robert has done her some special favours over the years – arranging and paying for her cataract operation and commissioning the stone to commemorate her nephew Archie, shot for cowardice in the war.

It's certainly true of Mrs Patmore that she is fearful of life beyond the kitchen. She doesn't seem to venture out into the world much and even within her own fiefdom, questions of happiness bother her less than those of duty and doing the job well.

But even Mrs Patmore has let down her guard once or twice. As she got older and retirement threatened, it was only natural that she should start to think of what life holds for her in her old age. When Joe Tufton came calling, Beryl – as she was, if only for that day – couldn't help but hope and dream a little, even buying herself a new blouse for the trip to the fair. She revealed herself to be as pleased by a compliment as anyone.

Sadly, it turned out that Mr Tufton wanted a cook more than he wanted a cuddle, and once she realised, she was quite relieved. But Lesley enjoyed having a boyfriend – 'brief though it was!... It investigated how she responded to that situation and it was interesting to see how it sent her off for a minute.' Most of all, says Lesley, she was delighted that although Joe Tufton turned out not to be all that he promised, despite her fantasy of leaving service to marry, she didn't allow herself to go too far off course, 'she wasn't a victim'.

The storyline about her nephew, Archie, also allowed Lesley to explore Mrs Patmore's values and gave her more of a back story. But most of all, it's the relationship between Daisy and Mrs Patmore that's been allowed to grow and has always been fun for them both – a close reflection of their off-screen friendship, too. 'I've always loved working with Sophie (McShera),' says Lesley. 'I've had some lovely scenes with just Phyllis and Jim, too, as the three peers together.'

Lesley's favourite line of Mrs Patmore's is easily recalled: 'It's you and me, Daisy – *contra mundi*.' She dissolves into giggles – 'At the time we didn't even

> **TUFTON**
> *I've not had food that good since the last time I were in London.*
>
> **MRS PATMORE**
> *I'm not just a pretty face.*
>
> **TUFTON**
> *This family's fallen on its feet and no mistake. I wouldn't mind eating food like that every day.*

Mrs Patmore is fond of a cap or hat, even a new blouse if the occasion demands it.

know what it meant (against the world)! But we say it to each other all the time now – "Ooh, you're being very *contra mundi*,"' and she laughs again. It's clear that Mrs Patmore is well-read, thinks Lesley, with her easy use of Latin phrases and Biblical references, 'Self-educated, probably,' she says, 'but I think she's a reader.'

The costumes have not exactly yielded a vast range – 'It was a step forward when I got into a pair of shoes, I'm always in these boots!' – but, says Lesley, 'I'm always comfortable. Once I got out of that corset – I never looked like I had one on anyway – life became a lot easier. I've always had the same cap, I think I once had a fancy one for going upstairs but that's it. A skirt for going out in, which has got slightly shorter over the years, and the fetching pink blouse for Tufton.'

The biggest challenge of the show for Lesley has been 'making sure you don't become sloppy because it's a very nice job, a lovely job. Julian says every year that we must keep an eye on the development of our own character and where we're at – they can't do it for us because there are too many of us. But getting new directors helps with that; they have different methods and a fresh eye. The responsibility is that the show is so beloved – the worst that anyone could say is that standards have slipped.' As for what next: 'It's all very exciting - who knows? Because of the show my life has expanded in all sorts of different directions and I've had experiences I would never have had. But I'll go wherever the work is. I intend to do it 'til I drop.'

Mrs Patmore was flattered by the attentions of local grocer Joe Tufton.

In 1925, Mrs Patmore looks little changed from the year we first met her.

MRS PATMORE

*We should always be polite
to people who are kind.
There's not much of it
about!*

Daisy

SOPHIE McSHERA

Sophie McShera was, quite literally, put in her place on the first day of filming by Alastair Bruce. He lined up the entire cast in order of hierarchy and Sophie found herself right at the very end. She's quite small anyway, so it was rather an intimidating start. But it was a key to understanding Daisy: 'She started off with just getting through the day,' says Sophie. 'You can relate to her because she's quite an ordinary sort of girl, one who reacts quite instinctively – that's how she gets into trouble. She doesn't have a side to her that she can hide it.'

The first day of filming is engraved in Sophie's mind. She recalls the shot of Daisy emerging into the hall, cowed by the high ceiling and beautiful antiques: 'I wasn't acting on the first day I was at Highclere,' laughs Sophie. 'I was with Rose (Leslie, playing Gwen) and I remember us being there and being excited. But it was intimidating driving up the drive. It's an amazing place to go into work. The next time I went, was that first shot of the series and I was on my own. It's a tricky camera shot – one minute steadicam – and it was like doing a dance, it was really well choreographed. It was exciting, the crew were excited about the shot in a technical way and in a character way it told you everything you needed to know about Daisy and the house.'

Having arrived at Downton Abbey as a young girl, Daisy is now in her twenties. 'She's had one of the bigger journeys as a character,' says Sophie. 'Just discovering things over the years. She wasn't educated and hadn't got anywhere at school, and the way she's reacted to the social changes has been quite different to the others around her. It's been so much fun to have that growth happen.'

While fond of Daisy, Sophie doesn't feel they are the same: 'I'm not sure how similar I am to her. I admire her a lot – her resilience, and she's really ambitious, I love that. It's crept up on me that she has this steely determination deep down. She's a quick learner, always managing to survive at the bottom. I used to feel sorry for her getting pushed around and bullied but it was waiting to come out – it's just that she was so young.'

Sadly, for a young girl like Daisy there wasn't much in the way of excitement when it came to her wardrobe, although Mrs Hughes's wedding provided a chance to dress up a little. But there are small pleasures: 'I'm out of my corset,' she grins.

The real journey for Daisy was that of her relationships with those around her. The romances – or not – that Daisy has had have also been fun to play: 'I did love the scenes with William, they were challenging and fun to film.' We know her back story is a sad one – she was not someone who was loved or cared for much, as a child. When Mr Mason took her in as an almost-daughter, it was more than she had ever had to herself. It did mean that she was fiercely defensive of him, not wanting Mrs Patmore to be his friend, too. 'I thought that storyline was really clever,' says Sophie. 'I understand where she's coming from. She's never had anything that's hers before – she doesn't have a family of her own, or her own house – just this person

> **MRS PATMORE**
> *Do you know, when you brought up that basket, I were so proud of you, I felt like crying out. If you were my own daughter, I couldn't be prouder than I am now.*

Daisy has grown from young girl to a woman in the six series, but her colours – as a servant – must remain muted in tone.

DAISY

I feel as if I've been down a coal hole and someone's opened the lid and brought me into the sunlight.

(Mr Mason) is hers and her sanctuary. Then it's diluted and changing. It's silly of her but it's understandable. He's like a father figure and a link back to William.'

Fortunately, the cook was more knowing than Daisy, as well as looking out for her almost as a mother might: 'Her relationship with Mrs Patmore has changed so much through that transition. She was a dogsbody and she's got a little bit of respect now. She's real friends with her.'

Over the years, Daisy has broadened her horizons. 'She wants to educate herself – they're all starting to worry and think about the future,' Sophie says. The teaching she receives from Miss Bunting and then Mr Molesley has a great effect on her. It's clear she was always bright but now the years ahead hold all kinds of possibilities for her, ones that she would never have even dared to dream were her right before the war.

'This was my favourite storyline of Daisy's,' says Sophie. 'I love how her taking the exams brought in these other characters and everyone had their opinion on it – Mrs Hughes wanted her to do it and Mr Carson didn't; and we found out about Molesley's interest in education.

'Daisy's got a strong moral compass and innate sense of what's right and wrong, and things can be a trouble to her, as when she saw (Mary, Anna and Cora) carrying Mr Pamuk's body. She feels she needs to do the right thing.'

Working in amongst the food can be a challenge, too. Not so much the technical side of things – you tend to see them just doing the beginning or end of dishes, rather than anything too tricky – but the tasty things prepared by Lisa Heathcote. 'The other day it was torture,' says Sophie. 'It must have been for a picnic or something dreamy for upstairs. There were scones and flapjacks, the smells were amazing and we weren't allowed to touch it because of continuity. Lisa kept trying to tell us they weren't as good as they looked, saying she'd made the scones heavy so they looked better and there was no ginger in the flapjacks! (Lesley Nicol) and I get really jealous of the servants' hall because they get to sit down and eat. I've sat down in that hall three times in six years and everyone else has their feet under the table!'

As for where Daisy goes from here, Sophie's fondness for her character is clear: 'We'll never know! The world's her oyster.'

Daisy's kitchen uniform has fine grey pinstripes to reflect her professionalism.

Mrs Patmore and Daisy visit Mr Mason.

Jimmy and Ivy must snatch a quiet moment where they can.

THE SERVANTS' WORKROOMS

INT. KITCHEN PASSAGE / BOOT ROOM. DOWNTON. DAY.

Alfred reaches the door and opens it to find Jimmy and Ivy mid kiss. He stands stock still. Jimmy and Ivy turn and look at him.

*B*elow stairs, viewers are most familiar with the servants' hall, the communal or relaxing area for the servants, and the kitchen. But there would also have been a warren of other rooms, each devised for a different purpose. We may not see all of them yet you can be sure they would exist in a house like Downton Abbey – a lamp room, boot room, brushing room, room for riding breeches, various stores, larders… Kinmel Hall, known as the 'Welsh Versailles', had a room purely for the ironing of newspapers, although at Downton that's done in Carson's pantry.

In these rooms, servants were able to complete a task with the necessary tools to hand, and out of the way of anyone else. Robert Kerr, the Victorian architectural writer, makes clear the importance of these quarters. Not only, he says, must the family have privacy and comfort but they must also 'have free passageway without encountering the servants unexpectedly; and let the servants have access to all their duties without coming unexpectedly upon the family or visitors. On both sides, this privacy is highly valued.'

It was practical, too – you wouldn't for example, wish to sew buttons on an evening dress in the same room that the shoes were polished. After the maids had finished their work above stairs in the morning, the rest of the day would be spent in the servants' quarters on other tasks – polishing brass, mending linens, cleaning shoes. These small spaces provided a chance for a brief snatch of privacy, a moment to talk to your colleagues under the guise of work, without being heard by the butler or housekeeper, let alone the family you worked for. When *Downton Abbey* first began, we most usually saw Thomas and O'Brien scheming in the servants' courtyard outside – a place so cold when they filmed the first episode in March 2010 that Siobhan Finneran's shaking fingers dropped her cigarette for the scene. But since O'Brien left for warmer climates to work with Lady Rose's ghastly mother, Susan Flintshire, Thomas must brood alone. Instead, we have moved into

The courtyard was where O'Brien and Thomas went to scheme, and Bates went to work.

the boot room, where we have eavesdropped (or so it feels) upon conversations between Molesley and Baxter, and Bates and Anna.

A built set at Ealing Studios, the boot room has also been used as Carson's bedroom, the post office and a bathroom. It is small, square and dark. Painted Grey Stone on the walls, as is the rest of below stairs (the hue is a popular Edwardian colour, using paint that mixes earth pigments and ground marble, a technique of the period), with the Indian sandstone floor. The room is sparsely furnished. Boots are lined up along one wall and above them hang peculiarly vicious-looking iron hooks. There's a sink, and a table covered with a cloth and tins of shoe polish. It's typical of many of the smaller kinds of servants' rooms that lead off the dark passageway.

If the door to this room or any of the others was shut, no one would be able to see much of what was going on in there. Possibly not even hear. All of which Mr Green used to his advantage, when he raped Anna. Dragging her from the kitchens, he knew – he had done it before – that in one of these hidden rooms, no one would be there, no one would think to look, no one would hear. As Dame Nellie Melba's operatic tones drowned out all noise and the rest of the household was entranced, Mr Green took advantage of Anna's isolation in a way which she could never have foreseen.

Thankfully Anna's resilience and Bates's kindness and love eventually saw them through this ordeal. Sharing her secret was Anna's hardest moment: a woman of her class in 1922 had only her reputation, her family and her career. There was every chance that had she not been believed by Mrs Hughes, Mary or her husband – as many, many women were not believed – she could have lost all three. And Mr Green's sudden death by murder led both her and Bates back to the York courthouse, putting quite the wrong people in the dock.

Anna and Mr Bates have had to conduct their entire courtship and newlywed days at work, so are well used to discussing their most intimate joys and difficulties as they polish shoes and go about their daily chores. While romances between servants were rarely encouraged, it can't have been too unusual a story in a house like Downton Abbey.

Fortunately, Anna and Bates have stayed together and as a couple seem remarkably able to look forward, not back. Their prime concern now is having their own family – of course, being as they are a couple in a television drama, this hasn't been without its complications either. And even though Bates and Anna work together, as their hours are long, it is in the boot room that they must find their opportunities to talk to each other about that situation. It was in there that Bates first confronted Anna when he believed her to have been using a contraceptive device, not realising she had been hiding it to save her mistress's own reputation. Such was the code of confidence between a lady's maid and her mistress (and a valet and his master, so at least Bates understood this) that Anna could not tell even her husband that Lady Mary had secretly gone to bed with Tony Gillingham.

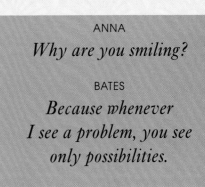

ANNA
Why are you smiling?

BATES
*Because whenever
I see a problem, you see
only possibilities.*

Molesley and Baxter have slowly but surely developed their friendship below stairs. It is the only place they can find to talk to each other during the working day. Above stairs, Baxter is usually found in Cora's bedroom; Molesley in the state rooms. Occasionally they manage to coincide their spare hours together, for a visit to Mr Mason's farm or a walk to the village.

However much an upper servant, such as a footman or lady's maid, may spend time above stairs in the large and spacious state rooms, for the most part, a servant was confined to the attic or the basement. Dark, small and unquestionably the property of your employer, they were not always entirely joyless but they were not places you could relax and call your own. For many, even those who had enjoyed their careers in service, to leave for a different world was to escape into the light.

Anna

JOANNE FROGGATT

Anna, former head housemaid now lady's maid, is our Christian, morally upright (but not *too* worthy), kind and generous soul at Downton Abbey. Of all the characters, she is probably the closest to perfect – which is exactly why Julian has put her through terrible turmoil. While he allowed her to fall in love with a man who fell in love straight back, nothing about their path has been smooth. Vera Bates blackmailed Bates so he couldn't divorce; Anna and her husband have both spent time in prison, falsely accused of murder; she was raped by Mr Green; and has even been inveigled into various deceits on behalf of her mistress including the embarrasment of buying her a contraceptive device from the chemist. Throughout it all, Anna has kept her composure and never remained anything less than completely loyal and loving to her own Mr Bates.

Anna and Mr Bates on their wedding day. Anna wanted to be sure to have become Mrs Bates before her husband's trial.

Anna has been promoted from housemaid to lady's maid, and has become a wife, but her dress has remained demure throughout.

ANNA

They call it 'making the best of things' and that is what we'll do.

We learned something of the reason for this in the fifth series, when it was revealed that Anna's father had died when she was young, leaving his young family destitute, and the man her mother subsequently married made intimate physical suggestions to her, until she was provoked into threatening him with a knife. In short, she is a woman who has been severely tested throughout her life.

All of this has meant an extraordinary role for Joanne Froggat (known to all as Jo) to play: 'I think she's pretty easy to understand. She's a decent person, she loves Mr Bates and she's a good soul.'

Jo won a Golden Globe for her portrayal of Anna as she suffered both the attack by Mr Green and its aftermath. In her research and also in the responses from the audience, Joanne was very moved by what she learned: 'All the letters I received were from women who had had the experience of either not being able to tell someone or not being believed. That shocked me – that so many people are still in that position of not

feeling they have a voice. I hoped it would be different today – it was a learning curve for me.'

Jo has been as keen a questioner of historical advisor Alastair Bruce on set as anyone, learning exactly what life would have been like for a woman in her character's position a hundred years ago. What has really stuck with her? 'That unless you were born into the aristocracy, there wasn't a great deal of choice for women. We're seeing that change little by little but we've still got such a long way to go – it's made me very grateful to be living in the present.'

At least, after everything they have gone through, Anna and Bates are still strong together and seem to have a long, happy future ahead of them – as does Jo. 'I think we leave Anna and Bates in a really nice place,' she smiles. 'I'm pleased with their ending. It's going to be strange (leaving the show) after it's taken over so much of your life, with the press and everything. But it's the right time, we'll go out on a high and we know we've done something special.'

Anna wears a silk two-piece the designer found in Paris. Everything she wears is delicate and petite.

Anna's closest friendship is with Lady Mary, who even takes her to see her own doctor in London.

BAXTER

Don't fish.
Especially where they're
never going to bite.

Miss Baxter
RAQUEL CASSIDY

Baxter had a chequered history before arriving at Downton, having been caught up in the spell of the conman Coyle. When working as a lady's maid at a house in London, she stole jewels for him and went to prison. Baxter has always taken responsibility for her actions, not seeking to excuse herself, but resolves that she will never allow herself to be that person again. 'She's not an innocent victim,' says Raquel Cassidy. 'She's having none of that. But unlike her predecessor she is essentially a good person.' And it is her friendship with Molesley that saves her: 'She comes so far away from herself in her dealings with Thomas (in series five), she dances very close to betraying who she truly is and what she believes to be right. But then Molesley is there as an unlikely knight in shining armour and his outstretched arm is what guides her back. It's wonderful how she reveals him to the audience.'

On the other hand, Raquel is quite different from Baxter – 'I don't think we're alike at all except that we both love our jobs,' she says. But she enjoys exploring the regretful side of Baxter's character. 'My favourite line is when she says to Molesley that if she could, she'd change her past for him. There are things she can't undo but what upsets her is the pain it puts him through. In that moment, she'd change it not for her but for him. I found that a very generous and poignant moment.'

Something that challenged Raquel in filming was the way in which people behaved to each other: 'The thing I find the most difficult is that they don't touch. They literally have to hide in these clothes. You can't even tug a sleeve. Molesley once touches Baxter on the sleeve and she has a look of horror.' Also, dare one say, Raquel is much prettier in real life. 'Although I have a fabulous make-up artist, I go in first thing in the morning looking pretty horrid and come out dowdy, and doing that for three years has taken its toll,' she laughs.

As Baxter is a seamstress her uniform contains fine detail.

Baxter wears a sailor-like outfit for a day at the beach, reflecting her off-duty, more relaxed mood.

Mrs Hughes packs up her bedroom and her old life.

THE SERVANTS' ATTIC

INT. CARSON'S BEDROOM/SERVANTS' PASSAGE. DOWNTON. NIGHT.

Carson comes into the room. The mattress is rolled up. The cupboards are bare. His old life is gone. He stares for a while at the emptiness and then walks out. In the passage, some of the doors stand open. It is nearly over.

Climb ninety-seven stone steps to the very top of the house and you will reach the servants' attic. It's not a place of beauty. There's little of the luxury or comfort that is lavished on the rooms below. In the summer it is tropically hot; in the winter, freezing cold. The bedrooms are sparse, furnished with a few well-worn cast-offs from the family – faded rugs, battered chests of drawers, one or two religious pictures. All the beds are single and most are two to a room. Hanging in the wardrobes will be a spare uniform or two, an outfit suitable for travelling in (usually a little frayed around the edges) and something for 'Sunday best'.

These rooms don't contain much but they are of great importance to the servants, as they provide a tiny bit of private space. For many, brought up in cramped cottages and probably sharing a bedroom with several siblings, these rooms will give them more space to themselves than they had had growing up. Personal touches are rare: a framed photo of a loved one back home or a book on the bedside stand. Few are likely to bother with even the homeliest of touches, such as a sprig of flowers in a cup of water, because these rooms are used only for the changing of clothes and sleep. Working in service was better in many ways than working on a farm but it meant you had very little time to call your own.

Even those like Carson – who have lived at Downton Abbey for many years – reveal little of themselves in these rooms.

INT. CARSON'S BEDROOM. DOWNTON. NIGHT. Carson comes in. A packed suitcase, lid open, rests on a chair. He stares into the glass. His old life is done.

INT. MRS HUGHES'S BEDROOM. DOWNTON. NIGHT. Mrs Hughes puts down her book and settles down in the bed. She too is thinking of the changes tomorrow will bring.

Woken with a sharp rap on the door at six o'clock in the morning by the lowest servant of the house (as we saw Daisy do in the first episode), the servants might come back up once in the day to change their uniform – the housemaids wear a day dress with a print, to hide any marks, for cleaning in; a plain black dress with a frilly apron for the evening. Carson and the footmen change into white tie in the evening – but otherwise they don't return until it is time to fall into their beds. Any reading is usually done in the servants' hall, in snatched moments between tasks. Last thing at night, after their late supper, with just a few hours to catch their sleep before their working day begins again, is not a time for any sort of private leisure.

There would have been just one bathroom for the male servants to share, one bathroom between all the female servants. We've had only glimpses of these – when Molesley (badly) dyed his hair and when Thomas admitted to Baxter that he was administering medication that had started to poison him. Now and then, we have spotted Bates with a towel over one arm, about to step into the bathroom – it leads off the same corridor of the bedrooms. This corridor is used for filming the attics as well as the passageway below stairs. By series three, even the attics had electricity.

At Downton Abbey, the servants are luckier than some – the family do not enter the rooms without permission. Remember how uncomfortable Mary was at the Duke of Crowborough's snooping in Thomas's room? However, this is not to say the rooms are the servants' own. Not only would it not occur to anyone to, say, paint the rooms in a colour they might like or furnish them with anything bought from a local shop, but everyone is vulnerable to inspections or questions from Mrs Hughes and Carson. Gwen, the housemaid in the first series, battled to keep her typewriter private, fighting the accusation that she was being secretive. She dared to ask who had been in 'my room', a point on which Mrs Hughes was quick to put her right.

In some ways, work as an indoor servant provided an easier way of life (outdoor workers mostly lived in cottages on the estate). No servant washed or ironed their own clothes as everything was sent to the laundry (although, of course, valets and ladies' maids had to clean, sew and iron their master and mistress's clothes, and a housemaid would be expected to help mend linens – almost anybody except kitchen staff needed good sewing skills). Upper servants would not even make their own beds. Nor did a servant outside the kitchen ever cook their own meals – something that rather brought Mrs Hughes up short in Carson's eyes when they began their married life.

Encouraged by the scheming O'Brien to believe that his affectionate feelings for Jimmy were mutual ('Alfred says Jimmy's always going on about you… soppy

MRS HUGHES

Now, see here. In the first place, none of these rooms belong to you. And in the second, I am in charge of your welfare and that gives me every right.

174

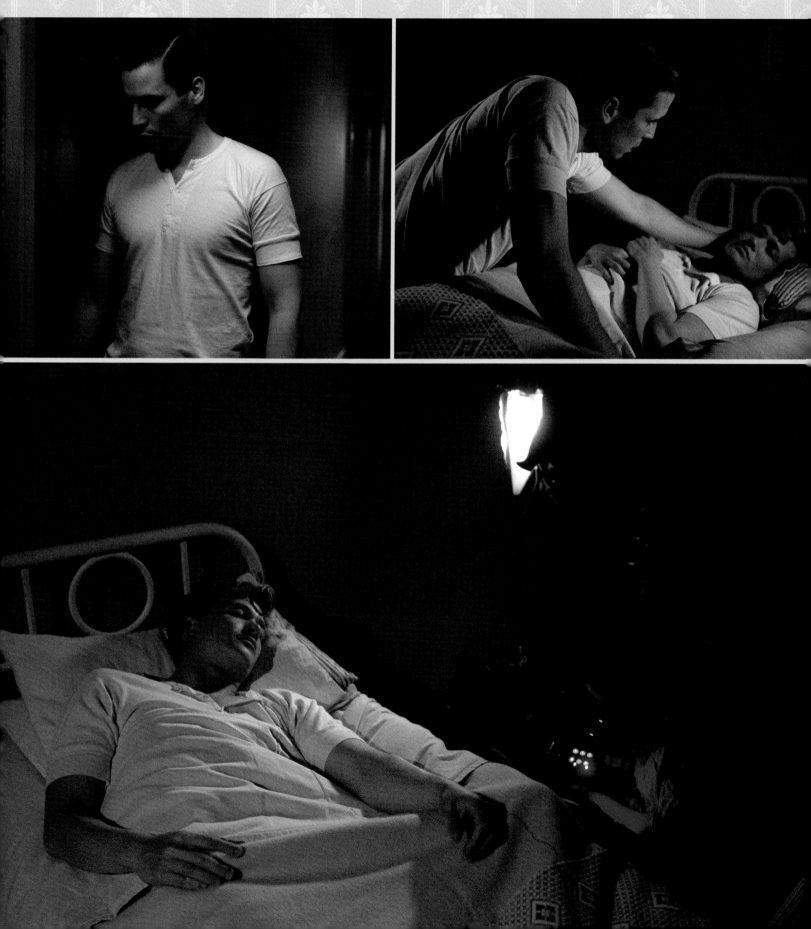

Filming a scene 'at night' can be done during the day at Ealing Studios, where the servants' quarters are a built set.

stuff, too'), Thomas Barrow was seen one night undressing in his room, riled and tormented by his desire, which had been repressed and simmering for months. Shirt off, we saw on his face a determination to do something about it at last. He walked quietly along the dark corridor and hesitated just a moment before turning the handle to Jimmy's room. Inside, lit only by the moon, Jimmy lay fast asleep. Thomas looked at him, walked across and bent down to kiss him.

Unfortunately, Thomas was not to know that Alfred was on his way back from a disappointing night out with Ivy and wanted to talk to Jimmy about it. Before Jimmy had even woken or realised what was happening, Alfred was in the room. Jimmy responded the only way he knew how – aggressively shouting at Thomas and telling him to get away. The fear he felt that he might be thought of as homosexual and that Alfred might think he had encouraged Thomas, made him hate his friend in that moment. And sadly, for Thomas, having a witness to his chanced kiss nearly led to the loss of his career and even imprisonment.

As it turned out, while Carson was deeply shocked by what had happened, Robert was more tolerant and saw Thomas's sexuality as something that was sheer bad luck – nothing he could do anything about. He didn't think that a good man should lose his job over it; Jimmy's campaign (or should we say, O'Brien's, as she was manipulating him all along the way) to have Thomas sacked ultimately failed.

But this was not to say that things ended happily ever after. Fair-minded though his employer was, Thomas was never going to be allowed to fall in love and marry another man in his own lifetime (homosexuality would remain illegal until 1967, when Thomas would have been over seventy years old; marriage between same-sex couples was legalised only in 2014 when he would have been long dead). Certainly in 1925 Thomas wasn't going to be permitted to openly pursue a relationship under the Downton roof.

The tragedy for a bright, ambitious man like Thomas was that he was stuck in his position as the risk of leaving and finding himself somewhere unsympathetic was very great indeed. Mind you, it has to be said that Thomas hardly helps himself – he has not always been the kindest of men. But over the years that we have known him, he has revealed a thinner skin at times than he might like others to know. He is a man trapped by his own heart and not in the way that one might hope for.

There was a fine line to tread in a servant's life when it came to romance within a household. Hanky-panky of any sort was, on the whole, forbidden. Carson and Mrs Hughes take it upon themselves to be the moral upholders of the younger staff, stamping out any friskiness should they see it. When you consider that a housemaid or hall boy starting work could be as young as fourteen years old, it is an understandable position. A maid who became pregnant would be sacked and would soon find herself living a life of destitution. We saw Ethel come dangerously close to this and it was only the intervention of Mrs Hughes that

Mrs Hughes admits her fears to her friend, Mrs Patmore, about what may be expected of her in marriage.

saved her. Perhaps she felt partly guilty, because she saw the maids' welfare as her responsibility. Mrs Hughes knew the presence of the flirtatious officers plus an empty bedroom in the servants' attic was a temptation too much to resist for an ambitious girl.

But for the older servants, romance was certainly allowed and for many, with so little time off, finding someone to love amongst your colleagues was the best chance you had. Certainly, no one begrudges the marriage of Bates and Anna, or Carson and Mrs Hughes. The beginnings of Mr and Mrs Bates's romance was in the servants' attic though only in the sweetest sense – when Bates took Anna a tray of food because she was feeling unwell.

Happily, this romance continued and now Mr and Mrs Bates live in a cottage on the estate. But with these two living out of the house, as well as Mr and Mrs Carson, the reduced numbers of servants living in with housemaids coming in from the village, it's only a matter of time before the attic stands empty, a museum to the life that went before.

Thomas

ROBERT JAMES-COLLIER

From 1912 to 1925, Thomas Barrow has been through quite a few different roles – from first footman to Acting Sergeant, then valet and finally under butler.

The character of Thomas was originally intended to be killed off at the end of the first series, but the producers found that they so enjoyed Robert James-Collier's performance as Thomas, they didn't want him written out. Thoroughly unlike his character in almost every way, Robert nonetheless perfectly portrays the smooth cruelty that Thomas is capable of inflicting. 'I like his ambition,' says Robert. 'He's very self-absorbed – in himself and his work – he wants to get to the top.'

But Thomas's character is a complicated one. In the very first episode he demonstrated this with no more than a look that passed across his face and yet imparted great sadness, after the Duke of Crowborough called off their affair with a callous toss of the love letters into the fire.

Later, after the war, Thomas sank all his money into a black market venture that failed when he was hoodwinked by the man who sold him the dodgy goods. He lost everything and was forced to beg Carson for a job again. Thomas had nowhere else to go and this point was driven home at the end of series three when Jimmy threatened to go to the police after Thomas's clumsy pass, unless Carson let him go. It was fortunate that Lord Grantham was more sympathetic and did not see that Thomas should have his life ruined for something he could not help.

> **BAXTER**
> *Well, I envy you. You don't care what people say, while I tremble at the mere idea of public ridicule. I should be used to it by now, but…*
>
> **THOMAS**
> *You're stronger than you think. And you're wrong. I mind what people say.*

With the arrival of Baxter, we learned a little more of Thomas – she knew his family and when she thinks his father is ill she says she's sorry, although Thomas says he is not.

Thomas's life has always been hard. An unsympathetic father and a sexuality that cannot be admitted. And then, in the final series, he realises that despite his many years of service at Downton Abbey, they are unable – or unwilling – to reward him with basic trust in his character. He only has himself to blame in many ways – over the years he has plotted and schemed against many in the house. His redemption, if one may call it that, is in his friendships with the children and the realisation that Downton Abbey is as good as it can get for him.

'In his head he can't be allowed to love,' says Robert. 'Eventually, society will wear you down with that amount of prejudice, when you're seen as abnormal and a freak. You can't be a stable normal person. Thomas alienates himself from people but even when he's being cruel, I feel sorry for him.'

What about Thomas's kindness to George, Sybbie and Marigold? 'He likes children – yes, that was a new one on me!' says Robert. But he thinks Thomas has an agenda even then: 'There's an element of keeping the parents sweet.'

Of the different positions Thomas has had over the years, which did Robert most enjoy playing? 'I liked the moment where he was briefly butler in the final

---

Thomas Barrow in his many guises from footman to soldier, valet and under butler.

series (when Carson was on his honeymoon). Thomas sat down and he didn't overplay it, he gave his orders politely. He made it even harder for Bates!'

In the end, it is Thomas's job that prevents anyone from asking too many questions, says Robert. 'Butlers gave their lives to service so they rarely marry, that protects him in a way. No one would see it as a strange thing.'

Has playing Thomas changed Robert in any way? 'In the second series, when we were in the battlefields of the Somme and Thomas gets a "blighty" (he deliberately gets his hand shot so he can be sent home), Alastair Bruce gave us a talk about war and explained to me that it wasn't a cowardly thing to do. Until you've been there and seen the horrors, seen the pain and heard the screams... That changed my perspective on the scene. What he put himself through was testament to how bad it was. It was a courageous thing to do. It made me tune in. What a privilege this job is – we're re-enacting these great heroes. It's taught me to appreciate things now.' Even filming in the recreated

trenches, on location in Ipswich, Suffolk, gave Robert a taste of how gruelling that life was. 'In the trenches, within two hours the soles of my boots were pulled off because the mud was so sticky. How could they cope with it? They saw man after man die. The most sane thing you can do is to blow your hand off.'

Thomas was not always accepting of his homosexuality and it became clear that it was preventing him from having even the friendships he wanted. 'He's not as confident and self-assured as we had thought,' says Robert. 'After Jimmy left, his ally in the house, Thomas realised that people are always going to leave him.'

Thomas's future may be uncertain when it comes to love and romance but he has learned his lesson when it comes to appreciating the things that he does have. Perhaps, too, those around him have learned that he deserves their sympathy and friendship. And we, regarding this with the benefit of hindsight, understand that the good old days weren't always good.

Thomas has a new Sunday best outfit for the sixth series as he is seen more out of livery.

Every evening, Thomas wears white tie.

THOMAS

I suppose I always wonder whether someone else is having a better time than I am.

The Estate
AND VILLAGE

The house is opened to the public for the first time in it's long history.

THE ESTATE

April 1912 – The sun is rising behind Downton Abbey, a great and splendid house in a great and splendid park. So secure does it appear, that it seems as if the way of life it represents will last for another thousand years. It won't.

*I*n the very first script, Julian brilliantly set up the tone of what would turn out to be six series of *Downton Abbey*. While the house is very much the centrepiece at Highclere, it is the surrounding land that sets it off as a building of real importance and handsome looks. Partly designed by the great eighteenth-century landscape gardener Capability Brown, the grounds have thickly clustered, noble cedar trees close to the house and throughout the park; there are velvet lawns, lakes – Dunsmere and Milford – temples and follies dotted around, fields of woolly sheep grazing and other bucolic delights. In the year 749, the land that now makes up Highclere was granted by Cuthred, King of the Saxons, to the Cathedral Church of Winchester. Later, under King Edward VI, the land was seized by the Crown, before passing it to another noble family. It changed hands several times before it came into the possession of the Herberts. At the end of the eighteenth century, Henry Herbert was created the first earl of Carnarvon, which was when the park was landscaped, follies were rebuilt, lakes were dug and so on. The boundaries laid down were quoted in *Country Life* magazine in 1959 and are so full of 'a remote and magical poetry', as the architectural writer Mark Girouard wrote, they are worth giving here, for a true sense of the land as it feels even today: 'First from Hilda's Barrow to honey way: along the way to Bregeswith's Stone: from that stone to sheep-walk: along sheep-walk to ale burn: along ale burn to beavers' brook head: thence to coferan tree: from coferan tree to the broad oak: from that broad oak to stuteres hill: downward: thence to the watch seat: from the watch seat to withy-groves: thence to sheepdell: from sheepdell to chapmen's dell: from chapmen's dell along the way: thence back to Hilda's Barrow.'

The house itself is approached by a long drive, giving any visitor whether on foot or in a car, the striking view of the extraordinary Barry exterior. Girouard gives the best description: 'With façades thickly scattered, and at skyline level encrusted with ornament… as a result the house has a net-like and almost lacy quality which makes it seem to shimmer with movement – an effect which is considerably increased by the shallow bowls of light and shade provided by the alcoves on the tower and east front.'

For a house such as Downton Abbey, several thousand acres would make up the estate, including a park, home farm, tenant farms, cottages, woods, shooting drives, lakes and gardens. Had Julian decided, a whole different series called *Downton Abbey* could have been constructed solely around the family and its estate workers, as there would have been far more people employed to work on the estate land than there were in the house. Waddesdon Manor in Buckinghamshire, which features in the second series as the exterior for Haxby Hall, the house Sir Richard Carlisle buys for him and Mary, had a head gardener, Johnson, who employed fifty-three staff for his department alone – fourteen of them worked only in the greenhouses.

Before the war, a gamekeeper would be in charge of rearing birds for the shoots, a newly popular sport for large house parties as we saw at the end of the

Mary flanked by her fiancé Sir Richard Carlisle and Matthew at the New Year shoot at the end of the second series.

second series, when the Crawleys host one at New Year. Tommy Taylor, keeper at Elveden Hall in Suffolk (bought in 1890 by the Earl of Iveagh, and still in the family), wrote in his memoir that by 1914 some 20,000 pheasants were bred annually for the sport, cared for by a complex system of under keepers.

In short, the estate was a miniature kingdom of its own. Most of the workers would be recruited from the village, with some of the specialist ones from further away, and they would be given their own cottages to live in. This presumably created a community amongst the workers – many of them would hardly have met any members of the family they worked for and would not feel any particular bond. But if they came from the local area, it may be that their family had worked for the Crawleys for many years and that in itself would have engendered a strong loyalty.

When the series first began, it was only Robert who returned this feeling of loyalty. Together with his land agent – a man as important to Robert as Carson – he would have known the situations of his workers, the wages they were paid and the number of years they had worked on the land. Gradually, Matthew came to learn how this all worked, followed by Tom and, at last, after Matthew's death, Mary. Now, with a more forward-thinking approach than many families, the Crawleys and their vast and sprawling estate have a better chance of survival than ever before. Mary is unafraid of tough decisions, whether it's cutting loose a tenant who hasn't paid his rent or selling land to property developers. Robert exercises more caution – he's the velvet glove to Mary's iron fist, as it were.

> MARY
> *We need to build something that will last, Papa. Not stand by and watch it crumble into dust.*

But before we get to the business of the farms and cottages, let's explore the gardens and grounds, which are after all the playground of the family. Downton Abbey's own gardens are not seen too frequently in the show, though there has been the occasional scene with Violet and Isobel or Cora, having tea outside. They would always sit in the shade, however – women at this time avoided the sun like the plague. Which is not to say that there haven't been some charming scenes – as when Edith and 'Patrick', the severely wounded soldier who claimed to be the heir presumed dead, apparently reminisced in one of the garden's follies. It was in the grounds, too, that Robert found himself talking to the maid Jane in a manner freer than he might have done under the roof of his house, leading to that fateful kiss later. Bertie and Edith filmed a couple of scenes walking in the garden. In the first it was a very windy day but was meant to be in the summer, so Laura Carmichael had some trouble holding on to her parasol!

Matthew and Mary had some of their most romantic moments in the grounds, as when he saw her sitting alone on a bench under a tree and engaged her in some

ROBERT

*My lords, ladies and gentlemen,
can I ask for silence?
Because I very much regret
to announce… that we are
at war with Germany.*

While Mary wrecks Edith's chances with Sir
Anthony Strallan, Robert shocks everyone with
news that Britain is at war.

When the Duke of Crowborough arrived at Downton Abbey, he took care to ensure that no one saw how intimately he and Thomas knew each other.

gentle flirting. The winning moment has to be the one that took place in winter, as they stood in the cold night, snow swirling all around them and he, finally, thrillingly, proposed marriage.

As is right for its size and position, the house has thrown the odd big summer party in the grounds. These events were an opportunity to invite local people from a variety of backgrounds, whether vicar or baronet, without having to worry about who was introduced to who or getting the social strata exactly right. Garden parties were generally an exercise in informality, a time to enjoy the sunshine and a glass of punch.

It was, then, this backdrop of summer and jollity that provided a contrast to the startling news that war had begun. This was based on a memory of Julian's father, Peregrine, who was only two years old when war broke out but vividly recollected a man coming out to read the announcement from a telegram during a garden party – he could only assume that the change in mood was so abrupt and fearful, even a baby could sense it.

But perhaps most of the action we see outside the house is right in front of it, on the expansively – some might say, expensively – gravelled drive. Important visitors, such as the Duke of Crowborough, General Strutt during the war and Cora's mother, Martha Levinson, are greeted by the senior members of the family and upper servants lined up by the front door. The general, in fact, was

> THOMAS
>
> *There's a war coming and war means change. We should be making plans.*

received by almost all of the servants, even the housemaids – although this was because the servants were part of the team that was running the convalescence for the officers, so it was important for him to see them.

Departures take place on the drive, too. When the Duke of Crowborough was hustled out, Bates was supposed to join him in the car to take them to the station, but Robert had a last-minute change of heart and asked him not to go. During the war, there was an emotional farewell when Matthew left in the car with General Strutt, William Mason saluting smartly on the drive and the family and servants watching as they drove off.

Crunching its tyres on the gravel too was Martha Levinson's white Cadillac, an American import she hired in Liverpool. The drive was also the first place we saw Matthew's handsome new car, brought back from his and Mary's honeymoon – later, the instrument of his death.

And in both the first and last series, creating a nice full circle, we saw the hunt standing on the drive. In all those years, from 1912 to 1925, very little has changed – the men are in their scarlet coats, the hounds are weaving in and out of the horses' legs, the footmen are doing their best to hand out sherry. The most significant difference is that in 1912, Mary rode side-saddle; in 1925, she rides astride.

MARY

That is why one talks to chauffeurs, isn't it? To plan journeys by road.

SYBIL

He is a person. He can discuss other things.

MARY

I'm sure he can. But not with you.

The other difference is largely off screen – in 1912, Downton Abbey's stables would have housed several horses. They may no longer travel by horse and carriage even in 1912, but they still used the pony trap – as we saw Sybil take Gwen to her job interview in. And riding for pleasure would still have been an enjoyable sport for the girls. But by 1925, they only get around in cars and Mary doesn't have time to go out riding for fun very often. As happened in so many houses, the stables would be reduced to make way for the cars and the groom that lived above them would no longer be there. Instead, the chauffeur lived over the garage. It was here that Branson worked when we first met him, and it was here that he and Sybil had their first, longed-for and illicitly thrilling kiss.

At Highclere, they still have their own beautiful double garage with a petrol pump, says Donal Woods. But they avoided dressing a set for stables – 'They've always brought the horses round,' Donal laughs. Otherwise, there's remarkably little for the production to do other than enjoy the natural beauty of the grounds as a backdrop for the actors' scenes. And so, on our small screens, may we.

A hunt provided a beautiful opening sequence for the final series, with Cora and Edith; Carson; Mary – astride rather than side-saddle, as she was in the first series – and Robert.

ROBERT

Goodbye, Mama.

VIOLET

Goodbye, my dear. Try not to let those Yankees drive you mad.

Robert returns home from America and (inset) all the servants lined up to bid him farewell, as he was leaving for several weeks.

YE 583

The estate farms rely on good management.

THE FARMS

MARY READS A LETTER FROM TOM

'I dreamt last night I was in the park at Downton, walking with Sybbie under the great trees, listening to the pigeons cooing in their branches, and when I woke, my eyes were filled with tears.'

Born and brought up in rural Ireland, it's easy to believe that Tom Branson would have come to love the land of Downton Abbey deeply. He has an appreciation for the rural way of life, an understanding of its rhythms and it's one that he surely wants to hand on to his daughter. It took going to America for him to realise it, but he feels at home at Downton. He still, after all these years, has some time to go to reconcile his position in the family alongside his socialist principles but the progressiveness of the era allows more flexibility on all sides than ever before. Even Violet has come to see Tom as the sensible, steady voice in the family and Robert finds to his surprise that he loves him, and is glad to have him back. It's not a situation any of them would have believed possible just ten years before.

Placing Tom as the land agent was a clever move by Matthew. It gave him a position that was considered reasonably smart. Traditionally, managing the estate was done by the master of the household and his land agent, as we have seen. No one else was involved and of course it did mean that if the heir to the estate was not particularly business-minded and paired up with a land agent who was not skilled either (in many cases it was an inherited job), things could go wrong. 'Instead of hearing about the land agent and tenant farmers, now we know them,' says Julian. 'It's less notional and more practical. I didn't want people to imagine the big house was owned by rich people and that was the end of it. It is a business. It's good to remind people that the agricultural economy is an economy and a great many people's lives depend on it.'

This was not too often a problem until the nineteenth century when a combination of increasing taxes and the agricultural depression required a steady hand to keep an estate on track. Robert's solution was, of course, to marry into capital that would fund any losses – that was where Cora and her Levinson fortune came in.

Farming at Downton Abbey is central to its very existence and survival. 'Part of the key of these houses is that they were employment centres, the focal point of the area, in the food chain and the local economy,' says Julian. Great estates had been self-sustaining for centuries by virtue of the fact that they farmed for their own kitchen and collected rents from tenants on the remaining thousands of acres, with no tax to pay. All that began to change in the nineteenth century and into the early part of the twentieth century, as income tax and death duties rose fast. There was also increasing competition from global imports, a lack of government subsidies after the First World War (which had been promised) and rising labour costs, all of which meant it became ever harder to keep estates like Downton Abbey profitable.

Edith cycles down to the Drakes' farm. This simple-looking scene required some complicated props: the bicycle, the sheep and the tractor.

Farmer Drewe and his wife gave Marigold a home at Yew Tree Farm.

Mechanical and technological developments also had an impact on farming. For example, the telephone and the lorry changed the way farmers did business – there was no longer any need to go to market, as they could close the deal with a merchant on the telephone and have the lorry deliver directly to the mill. In 1917, the government placed an order for 5,000 tractors from Ford, enough for them to become mass-produced and sold at £260 each, undercutting by some way British-made tractors. During the war, we saw Edith drive the local farm tractor for the Drakes, not a Ford but an International Harvester, also an American make. We can assume the Granthams were early adopters in this field – as they were with electricity, telephones and motor cars – probably because they were lucky enough to have the funds to invest in exciting new technical developments that would boost their output and therefore their profits. For many farmers, although there were increasing mechanical solutions to labour and cost, they didn't have the upfront capital needed to invest in them. In the 1920s, there were still 823,000 horses working the land in England and Wales.

Livestock farming also became an increasingly successful enterprise, particularly pig breeding. Mary and Tom were canny to branch out in this direction but they were far from alone. Pigs could be incorporated into just about any type of farm, large or small, and new methods of intensive farming made them a lucrative business.

The challenge for landowners at this time was to make their land profitable, but the temptation to sell up was an alternative too hard for many to resist.

Lloyd George introduced a measure that meant money earned from the sale of acres could be kept in the bank tax-free, while land that earned its keep was subject to heavy income tax, thereby encouraging estate owners to break up their estate. In Oxfordshire alone, two thirds of the estates changed hands immediately after the war. Foremost amongst the buyers were tenant farmers, who preferred to take a mortgage than risk a new landowner. The gentry thus gave their tenants the opportunity to buy their own farms, and so the estates were sold piecemeal. In 1914, 10 per cent of farmland was owner-occupied. By 1927, a third of agricultural land in England and Wales was farmed by owner-occupiers. It is exactly this fate that the Crawleys are working to avoid for Downton Abbey.

The tenant farmers of Downton Abbey might then have been grateful to be part of an estate that showed no signs of breaking up and with a reasonably benevolent landlord. Tenant farmers could often find that their farms were sold from under them when buyers wanted an estate intact so as to be able to farm on a large scale by themselves. By the 1920s, many farmers had come to realise that the fact they had been long, reliable tenants meant nothing when the landowners needed to sell.

DAISY

No farmer is his own boss. He takes his orders from the sun and the snow and the wind and the rain.

The farms we have seen on *Downton Abbey* have been filmed at a variety of locations. Yew Tree Farm, where Marigold lived with the Drewes, is shot at Cogges Farm in Witney, Oxfordshire. It's a thirteenth-century manor house with historic farm buildings and is rather grander than the production needed. 'The kitchen had to be shot in such a way as to make it look smaller than it actually is, to reflect Mr Drewe's working-class status,' says Donal Woods. When Daisy visited Mr Mason at his farm on a neighbouring estate, it was filmed at Stockers Farm House in Rickmansworth, Hertfordshire for the interiors. The farm is a Grade II listed building that originates from the seventeenth century. The exteriors of Mr Mason's farm (also used for Downton's own farmyard) were filmed at another listed building, Colstrope Farm in Buckinghamshire. Mary's pig scenes with Charles Blake were filmed at Hambledon Farm – the pigs being quite a complication in themselves. As the scene when Mary and Blake rescued the pigs from dehydration was supposed to take place at night, they filmed inside an enormous barn.

In the 1920s, great strides were made in farming technology and production but it remained a hard industry to profit from, particularly once the Depression hit in the next decade. Downton Abbey will have to remain flexible and innovative to pay for both itself and its taxes but, with Mary at the helm, it has the best chance it could.

Daisy and Andy visit Mr Mason in his home for tea; Daisy looks at the photograph of William in his uniform.

Tom Branson
ALLEN LEECH

Tom Branson arrived at Downton Abbey as the family chauffeur in the first series. When Allen Leech auditioned for the part, he was a Yorkshireman. He practised his Yorkshire accent on the London underground to Ealing but after he read the part, they asked him to read it again in his natural Irish accent. Julian had always intended to introduce the Irish troubles into the narrative so the producers asked Allen to play the part as an Irishman. Initially, he resisted – 'as an actor, you want to show off your range' – but in the end, of course conceded and as he has said, thank goodness he did as it led to wonderful storylines for his character.

So by the time Branson walked into the library to meet Lord Grantham, he had been written as a fully-fledged Irish revolutionary, with far-left views quite in opposition to that of his employer. He believed in the right to independent rule for Ireland, in the works of Karl Marx and in the abolition of the monarchy. Below stairs, he was not afraid to make his views known and when he began to drive Lady Sybil to her political rallies, he soon spotted a kindred spirit – and a rather attractive one at that.

But for all his strong beliefs in socialism, Branson was never violent. When General Strutt came to dinner, he never intended to harm him but to cause him embarrassment and discomfort by pouring a greasy, sticky bowl of slop over him. After he and Sybil had married and moved to Dublin, he found work as a journalist and attended rallies by the IRA. But he admitted later that although he had been a part of the movement that burned down the houses of the English aristocracy there, the sight of the families losing their homes made him realise that he had gone too far. In Dublin, too, they had lived largely off Sybil's allowance, which had made Branson even more defensive than

usual. 'It's a huge issue for him that he can't provide for his family,' said Allen of that script at the time. 'The fact that he's living off the very thing he's fighting against is very difficult for him.'

Forced to stay in England (he would have been arrested had he returned to Ireland), and alone with his baby daughter Sybbie after Sybil's tragic death in childbirth, Tom (as he was now known by the Crawleys) tried to settle down as one of the family at Downton Abbey. It wasn't easy. From his Catholicism to his abhorrence of upper-class formalities, Tom found

Tom's move from below stairs to above is reflected in his changing clothes. Although he resisted at first, in the end he has conformed, at least in the way he dresses.

Proud father Tom with his daughter Sybbie, a reminder of the wife he has lost.

BRANSON

I don't believe in types.
I believe in people.

himself having to adjust and compromise at every turn. As Allen saw it: 'At Downton, when he returns, he's neither upstairs nor downstairs. He's completely on his own.'

Gradually, however, he began to see the good side of the Crawley family and they in him. Firstly, he becomes friends with Matthew, even stepping in at the last minute to be his best man. 'He can relate to Matthew,' said Allen. 'He also came to Downton as an outsider. He's learning how to operate in that world. They have that bond.' But it is when he begins work as their land agent, drawing on the farming experience he had growing up, that Tom and the family become united in wanting the same thing, which draws them closer.

Funnily enough, Allen as an actor found the change quite as intimidating as his character did. Having filmed all his scenes previously at Ealing Studios, the atmosphere at Highclere Castle was completely different: 'I felt like I was in the wrong place. It all seemed another world.'

But what Julian made clear in his writing is that while everything was easy between Tom and the family once he was living and working with them, as soon as any outsiders came into the room, his disjointed position became palpably clear. Whether it was snobs at a cocktail party, the ambitious maid Edna, the haughty butler Stowell or the forthright views of Miss Bunting, Tom was constantly reminded that he was a round peg in a square hole at Downton.

Having Sybbie in the nursery made a big difference to the family's acceptance of him. For Violet, it was made easier by the fact that he eventually conceded it was easier to wear black tie in the evening than to have a discussion every night about his clothes. He was even able to demonstrate to Carson that he was able to play by the old rules, as perfectly demonstrated when he fetched his brother from the kitchen to dine with the family. But it was only when he went to America that he started to realise that Downton might have become his home.

Tom's suit here is in Donegal tweed, a nod to his Irish roots.

Tom's role as land agent gave him a purpose at Downton Abbey, and brought him closer to Mary and Robert.

Mr Mason

PAUL COPLEY

Albert Mason was first introduced to us as William Mason's father, although his character was off screen to begin with. We heard that William's parents were farmers, proud that their son had earned a position in service, where he had every chance of reaching the dizzying heights of butler. William was a kind boy who loved his mother and father but seemed to find that they wanted quite different things for him than he did – he would rather have been a groom, it was his mother who wanted him to go into service. When war broke out he longed to sign up but after William's mother died, Mr Mason was reluctant to let his only child go. Sadly, his worst fears were realised when William died from injuries sustained in battle.

> MASON
>
> *You have forty years of work ahead of you. Do you think these great houses like Downton Abbey are going to go on, just as they are, for another forty years? Because I don't.*

But Mr Mason took great comfort in his daughter-in-law, Daisy, and the two of them have developed a kind of surrogate parent and child relationship. Daisy had never had anyone look out for her and Mr Mason wanted the company, as well as someone to whom to leave his farm's tenancy. Paul Copley has lived in London for forty-three years but was brought up near a farm in West Yorkshire, which was something Julian knew about him from when they worked together on another television series.

Paul has much the same calmness about him as Mr Mason does and he seems to have enjoyed his part, dipping in and out of the show. 'It's a good story,' he says. 'He feels responsible for Daisy and she does for him. They rub along very well. I enjoy working with Sophie because she's such a sweet person.' Paul doesn't only like working with the actors: 'I had to learn to drive a horse and cart and Gemma the horse pulls my cart. We went to train on the paddock and I discovered that she's a star in her own right – she was in the film *Cold Mountain*!'

Paul also had to learn to drive a tractor but fortunately he has form in that area, having been taught when he was eleven years old. But the best detail Paul has learned from the period is, he says, that 'you do up the bottom button of waistcoats!'

Mr Mason and Mrs Patmore get to know each other better in the final series.

Mr Mason and his daughter-in-law Daisy have become family to one another.

Mrs Hughes in her new home.

ESTATE COTTAGES

MRS HUGHES: *I'm a trained housemaid and a housekeeper for how many years? And he doesn't think I can make a bed!*

MRS PATMORE: *You always knew he was too old to be trained as a husband.*

Our attention was first drawn to the estate's cottages as Matthew's pet project when he arrived at Downton. Having a large number of cottages on your land could be seen as a sort of status symbol – they might even be visible from the road, where your glorious house was not – but as they rarely brought much money into the estate, they tended to lie in neglect and disrepair. Most of them would be allocated to tenant farmers and those, lived in and looked after, would be pleasant. But those that happened to be dotted around, given over to either estate workers, retired servants or, very occasionally, married live-in servants, were not invested in to any great degree.

Matthew decides to change this – probably in part because when he first started life at Downton, he knew next to nothing about farming so could not meddle too much in those affairs. But working on the cottages was, as he saw it, a simple form of property development.

The cottages were fairly basic. Estate workers may not have benefited from electricity – there was no national grid until 1938, so these kinds of dwellings tended still to rely on oil for heating, lighting and cooking – but there were some perks. Gamekeepers might hand over the odd hare or rabbit, as well as pheasant during the shooting season. They would have milk delivered from the Home Farm, be able to keep their own chickens and run their own vegetable patch. Most of all, they had privacy and a place to call their own. This was especially important for Mr and Mrs Bates, and Mr and Mrs Carson.

Privacy, as we have seen, was lacking in the big house for servants and they even had to observe the formalities in addressing their own husband or wife while at work. But here in the cottage, they could relax and enjoy time to themselves, not at the beck and call of their master and mistress.

When Anna and Bates first arrived in their cottage, it was drab and dark. But they were able to give it a coat of paint as they had never been able to do in their

BATES

At least it doesn't smell damp.

ANNA

I think it's nice. Or it will be. When it's got a lick of paint.

Anna and Bates paint their new home.

rooms in the servants' attic. Encouraged, Anna may have taken to buying the odd bit of furniture or decoration when in Ripon or Thirsk – a clock, a small mirror, a tablecloth. They still wouldn't have much time there to themselves and getting to work in the dead of winter when it would be freezing cold and pitch black might have felt more of a punishment than simply walking down the stairs. But the pay-off was sharing a bed together every night.

Also breaking out of life in the big house to live in a cottage on the estate were the newlyweds, Mr and Mrs Carson. Not, as we have seen, that they found this an entirely easy adjustment.

Having lived several decades as servants, with all their hours accounted for, sleeping alone in a single bed, never cooking a meal for themselves or even having to dust their own room, living a shared life as a married couple in their own house hasn't come easily. Mrs Hughes has come to terms with her employers giving her orders – they do, after all, pay her a wage – but when it comes to her husband demanding that his supper be presented in a certain way, that is something altogether different. Carson, for his part, is used simply to telling others the way in which he'd like things done, and isn't used to couching orders in affectionate terms for a wife.

One can't blame either of them. Carson is a man who is both defined by, and draws comfort from, his deep attachment to the old ways of doing things. As the world has electrified, women have gained independence and the vote, collars have become softer, planes have started flying in the sky, monarchies have toppled… Carson has remained as firmly fixed in his views as he was in 1890. Mrs Hughes, however, represents what was happening to women in the twentieth century, says Julian: 'In 1840 they wouldn't jib against it but when you get a chance of change you start insisting on it, plates start to shift.' Even so, she's a progressive – Julian remembers his own mother in the 1950s hiding her efforts from his

The newlyweds adjust to being away from the familiar routines of Downton Abbey.

father. 'I remember her looking at the clock and saying – "Crikey, I'm on duty in ten minutes!" Being a wife was seen as a performance art and part of it was always looking great, putting on scrumptious feeds and the house looking lovely. You protected your husband from doing all sorts of things. There was a kind of pressure – when my father was in hospital [with tuberculosis], my mother took a lease on a house and thought she could get women in to clean it and paint it, but in 1946 there was no one to be had. So she did the whole thing herself, including having to get a bus to the Odeon cinema in Kensington where there was hot water so she could wash. It didn't occur to her not to do it. So when he came home, the whole house was painted and the drawing room was fixed and so on. She'd had the most exhausting six months of her life but the reward was him walking in and saying how marvellous it all was. They were playing parts.'

Furthermore, as Carson made very clear to a blushing Mrs Patmore, he wants a full and loving marriage with Mrs Hughes, with whom he is completely and certainly in love. Carson's frank admission was both unexpected and refreshing, but entirely in keeping with Julian's own feelings, as it turns out. 'There's something about embarrassment which is rather niminy-piminy,' says Julian. 'Certainly you shouldn't be embarrassed about the things that matter. My mother always said embarrassment was the only unproductive emotion, and I rather agree with her.'

As Carson and Mrs Hughes learn to shake off the ways of the big house and live in their cottage together, they will hopefully find a new lease of life in this different phase. Carson may miss the safety of the surroundings of Downton Abbey but he has enough romance in him to know that the risk he takes in having a married life instead is surely going to bring them both a far, far greater reward.

Denker attends to her mistress, the Dowager Countess.

THE DOWER HOUSE

VIOLET: I do hope you'll come and inspect my little cottage.
It was designed by Wren... for the first Earl's sister.

On the very edge of the estate, almost within the boundaries of the village, lies a pretty house that is perhaps modest in size compared to the centrepiece that is Downton Abbey. But considering that it was built with the express purpose of housing a single woman and her servants, it is generous indeed. It is, of course, the Dower House, occupied by our favourite stalwart matriarch, Violet, the Dowager Countess of Grantham.

As Violet's own domain, the Dower House reflects her character superbly with its period furnishings. The drawing room, which is really the only room in which we see Violet, is light and pretty, with a small bureau for writing her many letters. On this she has her favourite keepsakes, such as the precious netsuke and the paper knife given to the late Lord Grantham by the King of Sweden.

Byfleet Manor in Surrey, built in 1686, is the real-life house that provides the Dower House's exterior and drawing room (which has, for the last three series, been perfectly recreated at Ealing Studios). It was chosen, says Donal Woods, because, 'We wanted deliberately to pull Violet back into that Georgian world.' The Dower House was designed by Sir Christopher Wren, the architect famous for rebuilding St Paul's Cathedral after the Great Fire of London. It is to be expected that little has been done to the interiors since the 1890s, when Violet moved in, other than to occasionally refresh the paint. Even the curtains, if re-made, would be done in the same colours as before. Few inhabitants of such a house would seek to impose their own personal taste upon it. Violet took longer than the main house to connect to electricity but she has eventually done it.

It's a strange reward for a chatelaine, this rather lonely splendour. After thirty years as the Countess of Grantham, running Downton Abbey with her husband, not only would Violet have had to deal with the grief of his loss but she would have immediately had to leave what had been her home for three decades. Not

Violet interrogates Spratt about her missing netsuke.

The Dower House drawing room has been the scene of some prickly exchanges between Isobel and Violet.

that Violet would have seen it in that way, of course. She knew that to move to the Dower House was simply the order of things and therefore not something that one thought about, let alone contradicted or cried over. The earls, naturally, leave Downton Abbey for the last time in a coffin.

If asked, Violet would say that she lives at the Dower House quite, quite alone. But she lives there, of course, with the butler, Spratt, her lady's maid, Denker, the cook, Mrs Potter, and a housemaid. There are gardeners, too, though they are likely to live in the village. One consequence of having just two upper servants in the house is that if they don't get on, it can be war under the roof, as Violet has discovered. Both Spratt and Denker are old-fashioned, each with their own particular way of doing things and not at all fond of the other's methods. Neither, it has to be said, tries terribly hard to charm the other as each wishes to be the one to have the complete confidence of their mistress.

The wonderful joke with Spratt, that Julian has a lot of fun with in the sixth series, is that his stiff upper lip and appalling snobbery hide an inner life and background that he would prefer no one to guess at. Denker is not dissimilar – she may refuse to wash her mistress's smalls but she was happy to get drunk in a London casino. Servants, as much as their masters and mistresses, often perfected a veneer of Victorian sensibilities over a decidedly bawdy private life.

Strangely, for all her worldliness, or perhaps she just doesn't care, Violet seems ignorant of the servants' intrigues and Spratt's determination to protect his position. She quite unwittingly set Molesley up when she invited him to serve at lunch with Lady Shackleton in the first episode of the fourth series. Violet was hoping Molesley would impress her friend with his buttling skills, enough for her to hire him herself (at the time he had no work). Unfortunately, Spratt thought Violet was testing Molesley out for herself and tripped him up at every opportunity.

The house itself forms part of the Downton estate but is closer to the village. Too far for the Dowager to walk herself, she has her driver take her up to the house for dinner. Her daughter-in-law and granddaughters do walk down to see her but her most regular visitor is Isobel Crawley. Since Matthew died, Isobel and Violet have become if not quite what one might call chums, then certainly companions. In fact, when it looked as if Isobel might marry Lord Merton, Violet's unhappiness was not the threat of Isobel becoming a great lady of the county as everyone supposed – although I can't imagine the idea made her exactly happy – but the loss of a peer with whom she could talk freely about the family.

Violet enjoys her independence and the Dower House is an important domain from which she is able to summon others for interrogation. Even friends such as Lady Shackleton are not immune to being put under pressure, as proved when Violet tried to rope her in as back-up support for her hospital warfare. In fact, as many committee meetings for the saving of the cottage hospital were held in the Dower House as she could possibly muster. In earlier series, Dr Clarkson was put under pressure in the drawing room more than once: to admit that his treatment of Sybil would not have saved her life and to defend Isobel Crawley against Lord Merton's courtship. Violet is not shy of interfering in others' love affairs, as we know – whether to ask Lord Hepworth exactly what his intentions were with her daughter Rosamund and even to relight the spark between Sir Anthony Strallan and Edith (she later regretted that one).

We had a glimpse of Violet's bedroom in the fourth series – it seems almost improper – when she fell ill with bronchitis and Isobel took on the task of nursing her day and night, to prevent it turning to pneumonia. The set for the bedroom was simply the same one used for the drawing room, cut in half. The interior has been filmed from a built set, a recreation of the room at Byfleet Manor, since the third series. Most of the items in it are hired to match the original, and only tiny things have been changed – a couple of pictures have been added and so on.

In time, if Robert should die before her, Cora will come to live in the Dower House, and Mary will be the daughter walking down the drive to see her. George, when he is old enough, will join his Granny for tea and cake. And she will pour from the same silver teapot and use the same china. In these small ways, life as she has always known it will carry on, while beyond the estate it will continue to change at an immeasurable pace.

Violet hosts a luncheon hoping that Lady Shackleton will draw Lord Merton's attention away from Isobel.

Violet, the Dowager Countess
DAME MAGGIE SMITH

If there is any character that one might reasonably be a little fearful of, it's Violet. Not without due cause, either – she will deploy her considerable aristocratic hauteur when the occasion calls for it, whether you are friend or foe (and sometimes she doesn't distinguish between the two).

The indisputable matriarch of Downton Abbey, Violet has always called the shots. Only in the final series, when Cora took up the reins of the village hospital – the last battle won of many with her mother-in-law – that Violet conceded her absolute right to rule. Violet's relationships are key to understanding her: her rocky path with Cora; the fact that she loves her children, Robert and Rosamund, but is under no illusions as to their weaknesses; her closeness to Mary; that she managed to come around to Matthew and even Tom in time. Best of all, her sparring with Isobel. The only person unimpressed by Violet's haughty glare is Martha Levinson, the one woman who can find her 'soft underbelly each time', as she admitted.

But she is still 'Granny' and as is the grandmother's right, she will probably always interfere. Ultimately, most will agree that she does at least come up with the right answers – although Violet can be a snob, hankers for the past, believes the world was a better place when everyone followed the rules of social hierarchy and is bemused by modern mores, she is committed to her family above all else. Her fierce desire to protect her son and his daughters has led Violet to adjust to circumstances she would previously have dismissed as impossible: an illegitimate great-granddaughter, a chauffeur at the dining table, an heir to an earldom with a job, women with short hair, short dresses and the vote, electrical lighting in every room and her own son dressed like a waiter at dinner.

Violet was born in 1842 and would have had a Victorian upbringing: horses and carts, candlelit drawing rooms and allegiance to God and Queen before all else. The changes she has had to assimilate in her own lifetime are astonishing for their invention as much for their speed. At Downton Abbey, she was able to remain inured to many of these life-shattering

The Dowager Countess is always driven to Downton Abbey from the Dower House.

The Edwardian look is still Violet's preferred style.

VIOLET

I have a clarity of vision that allows me to resist the housemaid's trap of sentimentality.

developments until the 1920s when Robert started to pour himself a whisky in the library before dinner and the new world could no longer be ignored.

One cannot deny the romance of her youth, referred to at times in tantalising brief descriptions, particularly when she confessed to her affair with Prince Kuragin: 'We fell madly in love and in the weeks that followed, weeks of balls and midnight skating to the strains of the balalaika, we resolved to elope.' When Isobel asks if Violet ever strayed again, she replies that she never risked everything again. That's not quite what I asked, says Isobel. Violet's answer is perfection: 'It is all the answer you'll get. Remember, we were the Edwardians.'

It is Violet's bon mots and witty one-liners, as well as poignant phrases, that have defined her in the show. As Julian says, Maggie Smith is asked a lot of as an actress, as they require her to make the viewers laugh as well as cry, sometimes within the space of one scene. But it is her inimitable sense of timing that means sometimes his words are said by her with even better results than he expected. 'I write a line and think it's quite funny,' says Julian, 'then Maggie says it and it's hilarious.'

Despite her powerful presence both on and off screen, Maggie is a very generous colleague – all the younger actors attest to being terrified before working with her and then finding her huge fun the second they step onto the set. She, in turn, modestly downplayed her part: 'I think Julian has written an incredible piece of television. There are so many stories there with so many characters involved that it is a truly ensemble piece. It's not as though there were any individuals really – it's a whole company piece. And I think that's interesting. I think the viewers love to know what's happening in Carson's life as much as what's happening in Daisy's and Mary's.'

Of course, even Maggie had to admit that Violet's manner is a fundamental part of her: 'I think she's been imperious since the age of two and I think she's just about got the hang of it now. I also think – at least, I like to think – that she's got this sort of façade and underneath she's got a heart of pure custard. That's my theory anyway.'

All in all, Maggie has had a good time playing Violet: 'Yes, it is a lot of fun and she's a lot of fun to play because Julian has written some wonderful lines for me to say so it's all thanks to him really.'

Violet in one of the designer's most complicated costumes of the sixth series – it has about fifteen different layers and trims.

The difference in attitude between Violet and Martha is reflected in their dress.

The church has been the scene of marriages for the family and their servants.

DOWNTON VILLAGE

INT. CHURCH. DOWNTON VILLAGE. DAY.

Carson and Mrs Hughes, looking lovely in her coat,
stand before the Reverend Mr Travis.

Our very first sight of 'Downton Abbey' takes place in the village of Downton – in the opening credits of the debut episode, we follow the telegraph lines that run above the train that John Bates is travelling on, and then we see those lines connect to the village post office, where the postmistress is shocked by the message she receives down the wire. It is a nice illustration of the importance and connection of the house to the village – for centuries, neither would have survived without the other. As the world begins to change after the First World War, this becomes less and less the case. The feudal system upon which England was organised in the Middle Ages had the local great house surrounded by tenant cottages; the lord of the manor was the king of his own miniature kingdom. Even in this early twentieth-century period, Robert feels the responsibility of Downton Abbey to provide employment to the surrounding area – without doing so, his role and that of the house would be pointless, or as Violet put it: 'as useful as a glass hammer'. The village lies just half a mile away on the edge of the estate – the family and the servants only have to walk the length of the lime-tree-lined drive to reach it. It's no wonder the connection and the responsibility are so keenly felt.

In servicing the big house, the village would then have the resources to be able to service itself. Many villagers would seek work at the house and on its estate but the village had everything else that they needed, whether pub, school, church or shop. In this way, small rural communities were largely self-sustaining and only once roads were improved and the railways had rapidly expanded in the 1840s and 1850s, did this picture begin to alter. A modest village such as Downton could nonetheless run to holding markets that sold farm produce, village stores that stocked everything from tea and sugar to quinine and bloomers, a butcher, a chemist and a blacksmith. There's the church, of course, two pubs, the school house and even Downton's own railway station. It was busy and relatively prosperous, as we saw from the cars in the village square early

> **MARY**
>
> *You'll laugh at me but I've hardly ever been in a pub. Matthew wasn't really a pub man and Papa goes into the Grantham Arms about once a year to have a drink with the tenants.*

on in the show. Yet the feudal system still hung in there, if fainter than before – when Mary married, there was a great procession of villagers to celebrate.

The erection of the war memorial in Downton was a collaboration between the villagers and the Crawleys, although in choosing Carson to be the chairman rather than Lord Grantham, the villagers made it clear that they no longer saw their local lord of the manor as their natural leader. It was a sign of the changing times, as both Carson and Robert knew, and was equally unsettling for them both.

But perhaps the family was as much to blame. For while the family patronise the village by using the post office, the station and occasionally one or two of the shops, they tend to go to London for their more important purchases, while much of their food comes from their own farm and what does not is ordered from the bigger stores in Ripon and York. We know that Mrs Patmore prefers to order from the greengrocers in Ripon, the nearest town, rather than the village store, which probably wouldn't have had the specialist ingredients she needed, such as fresh ginger. In short, the village was supported by the family but it was not their place for rest and recreation – that was for the servants.

The Grantham Arms is occasionally used by the family, although it does seem that any time they are there it is for a rather suspect reason. Tom stayed in the pub while waiting for Sybil to join him so they could run away together but was intercepted by Robert, who attempted to pay him off with a cheque – it was, naturally, steadfastly refused. Later, when Tom said he was going to the pub for lunch (the family were away in Scotland), the scheming maid, Edna Braithwaite, made sure she was there first, so that he would feel obliged to join her; a woman drinking alone in a pub would have seemed very racy indeed.

As the servants have so little time off – usually from four o'clock until ten o'clock one day a week and every other Sunday for the same hours – they are not able to travel far to spend their free time so instead rely on whatever the village can provide. Mostly, of course, this is about the pub. If not the Grantham Arms then the Dog and Duck (where Carson was spotted by Bates, illicitly dropping off food for Charlie Grigg in the first series), although any servant has to watch that Carson or Mrs Hughes does not smell alcohol on their breath – it might not be grounds for dismissal but it would be strongly frowned upon. 'Drunkenness was looked down on from a great height,' says Julian.

The real fun comes when the fair is in town. We saw this in the first series – there were tents for stalls, a helter-skelter, a steam-run pianola, a coconut shy. The fair used for the filming is a vintage one that still runs today. Such a fair would travel around the country, arriving in the same places at the same time every year.

Carson allowed all the servants to go the Downton Fair – William, Gwen, Thomas and Daisy. Meanwhile Mrs Hughes had agreed to accompany her old flame, Joe Burns.

The Downton annual cricket match – House versus Village.
Molesley was out first ball but thanks to a brilliant catch by Tom
at the last, the House won.

As with any fair today, it was for nothing more than simple pleasure – although the cost was considerably less. A penny a ride or for a go at the hoopla.

The annual summer cricket match between Downton Abbey and the village was another highlight of the year. It was an occasion for the house, servants, estate workers and villagers to come together on the well-maintained pitch (which was why Robert was highly reluctant to give it up for the war memorial and did ultimately win that battle). Master and servant found themselves on the same team and they all took it seriously – especially Molesley, who talked rather a better game than he actually played. Meanwhile, those not playing were able to enjoy the simple pleasures of sunshine, strawberries and cream, and the quintessential English sound of leather on willow.

All of the village scenes are filmed in Bampton, Oxfordshire. A pretty place, with buildings of Cotswold stone, it has welcomed a huge number of tourists since its alliance with Downton Abbey began. In the village is the exterior of the Grantham Arms, which is, in fact, a house with a sign put up by the film crew – the owners left the sign up for a while as they liked it but eventually had to take it down as so many people kept knocking on the door and asking if they could come in for a pint. The servants of the house aren't often seen going for a drink here but there have been one or two occasions where it has served as the setting for a clandestine meeting – such as when Mrs Hughes met her former sweetheart, Joe Burns.

The church, which has been renamed for *Downton Abbey* from St Mary's to St Michael and All Angels, has been the scene of several pivotal moments. In the very first episode, we saw the memorial for Patrick and James Crawley, with a horse and trap trotting down the road – a reminder of the Edwardian times in which the characters still lived, despite the encroachment of modern life. Here, too, was Lavinia's funeral, her gravestone a constant reminder to Matthew as he walked through the village to his mother's house. Shortly afterwards, it was in the church graveyard that Mary found Isobel and Matthew, and the three of them prayed for Lavinia. After Mary had walked off, Isobel told Matthew that it was clear she was still in love with him but he wouldn't hear it – he believed his fiancée had died of a broken heart thanks to the two of them, and that they both deserved to be unhappy.

Fortunately, he didn't stick to his guns on this occasion and allowed himself to be persuaded round – it wasn't long until we had the happy scene that saw the two of them in church for their wedding. Many families in those days, whether they lived in the village or the big house, would see their lives revolve around the same church – from their christening, to their marriage, their children's christening and finally, their own funeral. It made churches a very significant part of an individual as well as collective life. So it was that Matthew's own funeral was held here, too, if far too many years sooner than he would have wanted.

Mary cautiously approaches the guilt-ridden
Matthew at the funeral of his fiancée Lavinia Swire.

Carson and Robert at the unveiling of the war memorial.

It's symbolic of a certain way of life then that the church in which Mary was baptised and married, should also be the one in which she buried her husband. No matter what life flung at you – birth, death and everything in between – the one constant was place, your home, your village, your church. This was emphasised when the Downton war memorial was erected in the middle of the village – it demonstrated that those who had lived at Downton and died for their country were still a part of the collective memory and mourning.

Another centre of village life was the shop. As rail travel and roads increased in the Victorian era – not to mention refrigeration – transportation of meat and dairy products became more commonplace, so villages gradually came to support a greater number of specialist shops. But there was usually one 'general store' that tried to stock just about anything one could think of. There have been few scenes filmed in shops but we know the family bought things locally, such as Violet's bottle of scent. We have seen a number of scenes in the post office – as when Bates sent off the money for his leg contraption, the housemaid Gwen posted the papers for her secretarial course and Lady Rose placed an ad for a new lady's maid for Cora.

By the 1920s, the great improvement for the shop owner and their customers was the arrival of pre-packaged items. Before that, goods were ordered (and often bought) in bulk – a shopkeeper's skill lay in getting things in for the best price, then processing them for sale by, say, roasting and grinding the coffee, mixing the herbs, cutting and crushing the sugar. For the more unscrupulous, the temptation at this stage was to adulterate the stock – commonly adding chalk to flour, brick dust to chocolate, sand to coffee and sheep dung to tea. Something that Thomas found to his cost when he dabbled in the black market after the war.

The school house is, of course, also located in the village. This was the workplace of Miss Sarah Bunting, the socialist teacher who fell for Tom Branson, and was

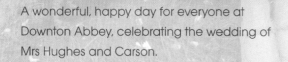

A wonderful, happy day for everyone at
Downton Abbey, celebrating the wedding of
Mrs Hughes and Carson.

also paid by Mrs Patmore to teach Daisy. An educated, lower-middle-class woman, she proved too radical even for Tom and decided to leave the village, but it is likely that a woman like her would have gone on to a long, successful teaching career. For many years, this would have been the only school for all the children that lived close by, probably run by a single schoolmistress and her young assistant, with nothing but a thick curtain to divide it into two rooms – one half for the younger children, the other for the older. The 1918 Education Act raised the school leaving age from twelve to fourteen, thereby improving the elementary education that had been in place. Perhaps at this point, the village school at Downton improved too, with Miss Bunting and then Mr Dawes on the teaching staff.

All children were taught the basic skills of reading, writing and arithmetic (referred to as the 'Three Rs'). With the increase of socialism and changing ambitions, education became seen as a right for all. But the working classes still received the worst education. There were grammar schools for the clever but while these were free, uniforms, books and other equipment were not – sometimes affording these proved prohibitive for their families. The upper classes were educated at expensive private schools, usually boarding, if not by governesses at home. Very, very few working-class children went on to university – the system in which they were educated did not encourage it.

As a large building in the middle of the village, the school house is occasionally used for other purposes – most cheerfully, for the occasion of celebrating Mrs Hughes and Carson's wedding. (The school house was not filmed at Bampton but at Burghclere Village Hall.) The great pleasure of this was partly that it was one of the very few occasions that we were able to see the servants all dressed up. Being below stairs, the actors are rarely out of their uniforms, which makes for fewer fittings with the costume department but does mean they perhaps miss out slightly on the fun of new frocks. Sophie McShera, as Daisy, has just four dresses (two for winter, two for summer), two coats and two hats. But for the wedding, Daisy would have been keen to wear something new. Carson in his Prince of Wales check suit was a very fine sight to see.

Although the village of Bampton looks remarkably untouched by modern life even today, which makes it ideal for filming a period drama, and the villagers themselves have always been extremely welcoming and co-operative (many have had parts as extras in the crowd scenes), it hasn't been without its difficulties. Not long before filming was due to start at the very beginning, the wall in the main street collapsed – so *Downton*'s own art department rebuilt it. And then, a matter of days before filming commenced, a huge amount of scaffolding was erected around the church. Director Brian Percival carefully shot around it so that it wasn't on screen, rather than rely on post-production techniques to delete it. But the village has enjoyed other, surprising, benefits to the presence of the film crew – such as the guttering that has had a fake brickwork cover put over it. Time, it seems, can be turned back when you have an art department on hand.

Behind the scenes in Bampton. A relaxed picnic and a game of cricket for the servants.

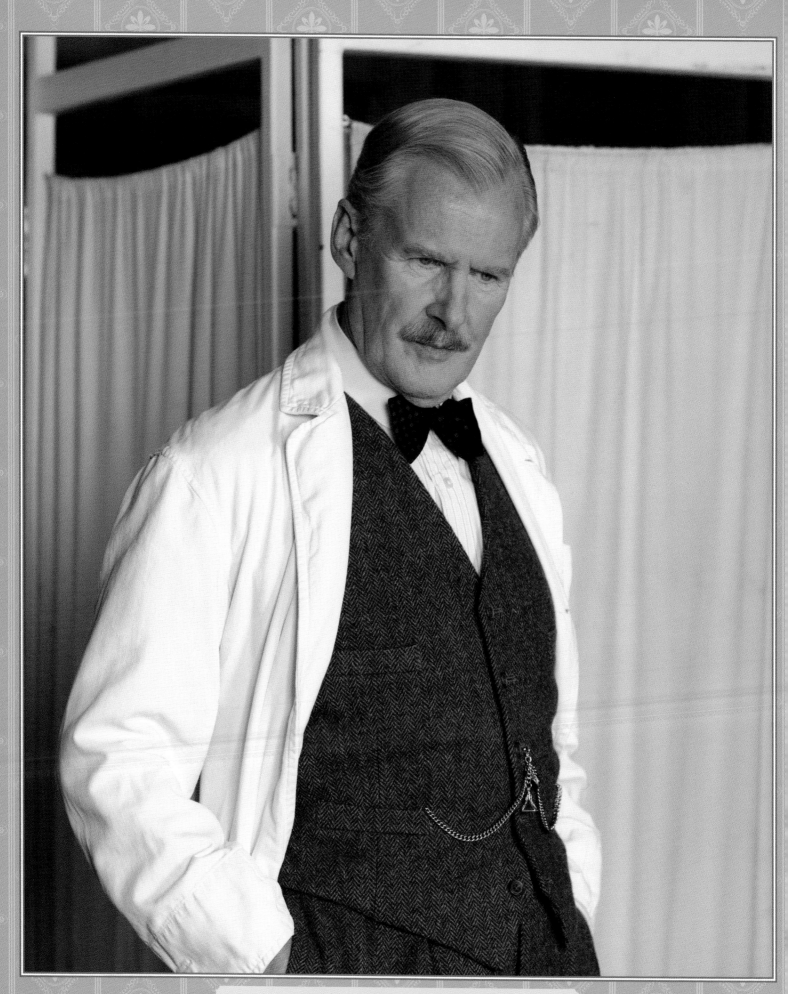

Dr Clarkson consults at Downton Hospital.

DOWNTON COTTAGE HOSPITAL

CLARKSON: Nurse Crawley, I may not be your social superior in a Mayfair ballroom, but in this hospital I have the deciding voice.

For all that appears to be pleasant and graceful in the 'good old days' there are two reasons most of us would be reluctant to return to the past, even if you could be guaranteed a life above stairs rather than below: medicine and dentistry.

While the Crawley family rely on their doctors in Harley Street, London, for any serious health matters, the servants, the estate workers and the villagers are all dependent upon the cottage hospital. As we head into the 1920s, this is beginning to change, as we see with the plot line in the final series, in which the bigger hospital at York takes over its control, meaning that Dr Clarkson is no longer managing the most serious medical cases. Given the number of misdiagnoses and his reluctance to embrace modern methods, perhaps this is no bad thing…

After the war and the global influenza epidemic, healthcare began to improve, if sporadically – the standard of care a person received depended greatly on their class, income, employment status and where they lived in the country. The Ministry of Health – of which department Neville Chamberlain was minister in his visit to Downton Abbey in the sixth series – was established only in 1919 and had the responsibilities of public health, housing, the Poor Law, hospitals and infirmaries.

Prior to the establishment of the National Health Service in 1948, any kind of medical care had to be paid for. There was a system of health insurance introduced in 1911, to which employers and beneficiaries had to contribute, which allowed a certain amount of treatment to be covered. Otherwise, there was a mix of private voluntary trusts (which provided 25 per cent of all hospital beds) and public hospital provision – but as these were un-coordinated, the system was erratic and serious illness could ruin a poor family. Children were still very prone to sickness although fewer died from epidemics than before the war. Laurie Lee, author of *Cider With Rosie*, wrote that his first year was plagued by 'diphtheria, whooping cough, pleurisy, double pneumonia and congestion of the bleeding lungs'.

A cottage hospital like the one we have at Downton – that is, a local hospital that serves a village and its immediate surrounding areas – would provide free healthcare for those on a low income. This would mean that the hospital was very reliant on fundraising efforts and public subscriptions to get by. This was the reason that a local chatelaine – such as the Dowager Countess – would usually be appointed President. It was important to have at the top someone who could best persuade others to donate their money.

As the locale of medical concerns, the Downton hospital has had its fair share of drama. From Julian's point of view, he was able to have the family close to this drama through the involvement of Isobel Crawley. Where Violet had been a proud President and jolly useful, no doubt, as a fundraiser, it was clear from the moment she arrived that Isobel wished to be more hands-on as Almoner. Not only was Isobel's late husband, Reginald Crawley, a doctor but she herself had trained as a nurse. She comes from a proud line of medical practitioners – her father, Sir John Turnbull, was a surgeon. Not that Violet cares too much for that, but in the modern world being well-educated makes Isobel a more progressive person than the rest of her peers.

CLARKSON

I must compliment you, Mrs Crawley. When you made your offer I thought you might be a 'great lady nurse' and faint at the sight of blood. But I see you're made of sterner stuff.

When Isobel first arrived and interfered with his treatment of Farmer Drake, who was suffering a bad case of dropsy, Dr Clarkson did not take kindly to her. Isobel was by that stage already on the hospital board but the general expectation was that she would be a 'great lady' as Dr Clarkson said, more used to mopping brows than blood. Nurses even into the 1920s were still struggling to be recognised as professional rather than 'caring' – state examinations were not introduced until 1925. But, as we have seen, she is not only knowledgeable but brave and during the First World War, when she found she was unable to occupy a role of any real consequence at home, she left to work for the Red Cross in France. This would have exposed her to some truly terrible scenes of suffering, made all the more appalling by the knowledge that her only son was fighting close by.

Downton Abbey wears no rose-tinted spectacles when it comes to the gut-wrenching difficulties of medical diagnosis and treatment. And Downton hospital was far from exempt from the horrors of the war. The huge, unexpected numbers of severely wounded soldiers put a strain on hospitals all over the country. As soon as men could be released from military hospitals close to the frontline, they would be sent back to their local medical centre, which at least meant that their families could visit them. But sleepy village hospitals that had had largely to deal

The terrible injuries that Matthew suffered in the war broke the
hearts of his mother, Isobel, and Mary.

with nothing more complicated than childbirth and the deaths of old people were suddenly swamped by men suffering multiple and terrible wounds. It brought the war closer to home and meant the scythe of death was a tangible presence almost anywhere you lived – only forty villages in the whole of Britain escaped losing some of their young men in the war.

But it was a complex time for medicine as war escalated the need for advances in anaesthesia, surgery and post-operative treatments as the wounded arrived in vast numbers. As well as the physical injuries, the war, arguably, forced doctors to face up to the emotional devastation as soldiers suffered from shellshock and depression – what we would now call post-traumatic stress disorder.

In the garden of the village hospital Dr Clarkson, Nurse Sybil and Corporal Barrow assist Edward Courtenay, the gas-blinded soldier.

In the second series, we saw Nurse Sybil and Corporal Barrow visibly moved by the plight of the soldier Edward Courtenay, blinded by mustard gas; he killed himself. As the village hospital was unable to keep men who had recovered from the worst of their injuries as the beds were needed, the plan was then formed to turn Downton Abbey into a convalescent home for officers. This was not unusual – in fact, Highclere Castle was a hospital in the First World War, with one of the bedrooms used as an operating theatre.

During the war, of course, Matthew was severely injured, leaving him unable to walk for a while. After his initial treatment and assessment in a field hospital, Matthew was sent to Downton where Dr Clarkson was unable to do much more than confirm the previous doctor's prognosis. Fortunately they were both wrong. The injuries that came with this bloody war, with its intense fighting and use of tanks and aeroplanes, brought complications that doctors had almost never seen before. Medical science fought hard to keep up but the escalating violence was often beyond them – a misdiagnosis was hard to avoid at times.

A few years later a heavily pregnant Mary rushed home from Scotland, feeling tired and unwell. In fact she was experiencing the twinges of an early birth and so George was born at Downton hospital. Mary would have preferred to do as most of her friends would have done, which was to have given birth in her room at home, possibly with a London doctor in attendance. But given the raw experience the family had had with Sybil at the hands of the pompous Sir Philip Tapsell, Mary may have preferred to be with Dr Clarkson anyway. In any case, Julian set it up so that we had the touching, loving scene in the hospital with just Matthew, Mary and their new baby, minutes before Matthew was killed.

The exterior shots of the hospital are filmed at Bampton Library – it was previously the old grammar school building. The interior is a built set and for the final series this set was made on location as the production team had run out of space at Ealing Studios. An authentic 1920s X-ray machine, which was difficult to find, was brought in for filming and an expert found to teach the actors how to use it correctly.

In the 1920s, as medical science continued to improve and new discoveries were made at a rapid rate, the question of whether local doctors such as Dr Clarkson could bear the responsibility of decisions for seriously ill patients in their cottage hospitals was hotly debated. For those who resisted change, it was symbolic of the old ways of life coming to an end and they fought against it fiercely. It was, you might say, a matter of life and death.

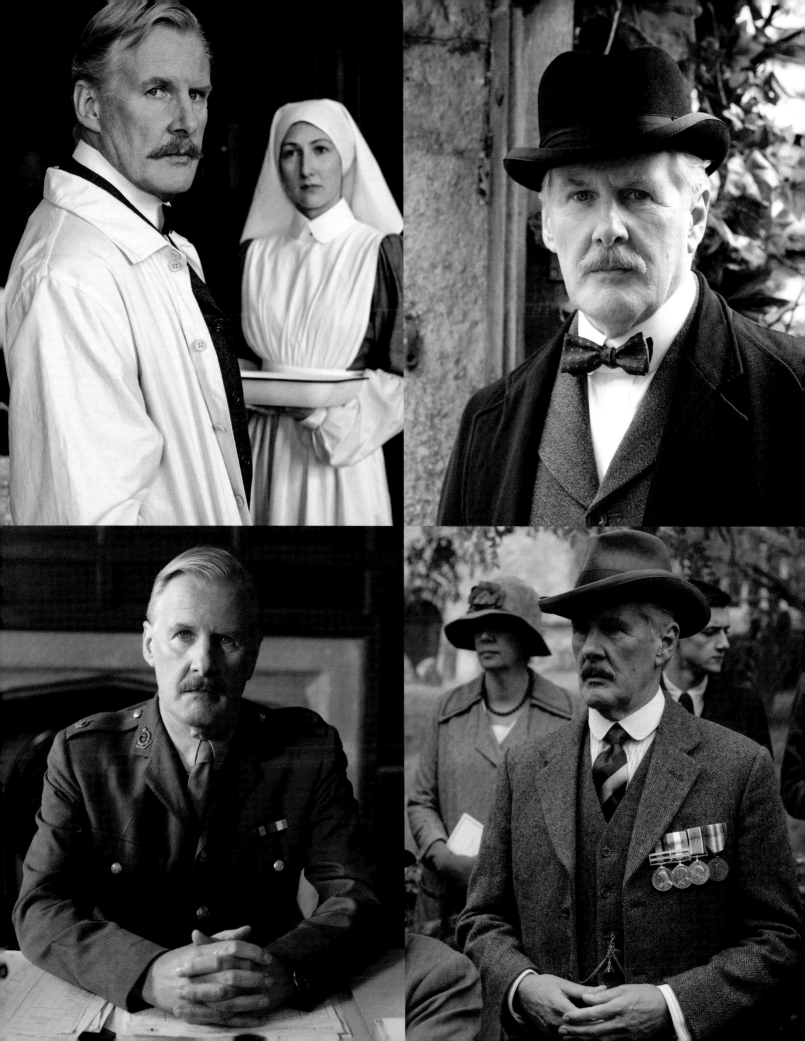

Dr Clarkson

DAVID ROBB

We first met Richard Clarkson when he clashed with Isobel Crawley over her suggestions for treating Farmer Drake for dropsy. Over the years, the village's doctor has not had an easy ride, often finding himself caught in the middle between his hospital's benefactress and President, the Dowager Countess, and the forthright manner of Isobel Crawley. Not to mention a run of rather unfortunate misdiagnoses – from Farmer Drake's treatment to Matthew Crawley's bruised spine. The actor, David Robb, eventually got quite fed up with his character always getting it so spectacularly wrong and asked Julian for a chance to get it right. Julian gave it to him in the storyline about Sybil's death in childbirth, where Dr Clarkson's correct diagnosis of eclampsia might have saved her life had the so-called expert from Harley Street, Sir Philip Tapsell, not ignored him.

David thinks his character might have been a doctor in the army during the Boer War and at Downton was more or less a retired GP. He also thinks that while he wants success in his work, he is not ambitious: 'He's not stupid but he is a bit of a plodder,' says David. 'He's very honourable and always does what he thinks is right but it isn't always the case. Things are changing but he's getting older and he's not cutting edge.'

In series three, we saw Dr Clarkson nearly propose marriage to Isobel at Thirsk Fair – he believed the two of them to be well matched in their medical interests and attitudes to class. He certainly bristled when Lord Merton arrived on the scene. But he's a reasonable, pragmatic man and conceded graciously when he realised that Isobel wouldn't turn to him instead, even joining her team when it came to the battle over the village hospital in the final series.

The doctor has worked closely with the Crawley family for many years.

Dr Clarkson finds himself again in the middle of an argument between Violet and Isobel.

Matthew waves goodbye as he returns to war.

DOWNTON STATION

MARY: *It's my lucky charm. I've had it always.*
So you must promise to bring it back...
without a scratch.

For Julian Fellowes and composer John Lunn, their favourite scene in the entire *Downton Abbey* oeuvre takes place at Downton Station. Early in the morning, Mary goes to see Matthew before he catches his train back to London and then on to the trenches in France. He has been home on leave, and introduced her to his fiancée Lavinia Swire – it had been the first time that Matthew and Mary had seen each other for over two years, since they had broken off their own near-engagement. On seeing him, it was painfully clear to the audience that they still loved each other but were now unable to be together. When Mary went to the station to say goodbye she was acting on advice from Carson, who told her to let him know she loves him. When it comes to it, she couldn't quite bring herself to tell him the truth but she knows that it could easily be the last time she ever sees him. Thousands upon thousands of young men were dying in the war and officers had an average life expectancy of six weeks on the front line. So she gave him her lucky charm, an old toy dog (it was originally written in the script as a toy rabbit but the prop was deemed too girly, so it was changed at the last minute) and wished him the very best of luck. It is in their restraint, their stoicism – Matthew facing almost certain death, both holding a love for the other that cannot be expressed – that the scene becomes almost unbearably moving. Julian says even now, having seen it many times, it never fails to bring a tear to his eye. John Lunn recalls showing the scene to film students for a lecture on composing scores – he screened the scene with the music and without, the lesson intended to show what the music could do to strengthen the mood. Only as he watched it he realised that it was one of those times when the images said it all. 'The difference wasn't big enough! It's a really good scene.'

Deliberately in parallel to this parting, just one episode later, Mary is shown saying goodbye to Sir Richard Carlisle on the platform. The self-made newspaper

Mary says goodbye to Sir Richard Carlisle.

baron is in love with her but it's clear that this is an entirely different relationship. He proposes to Mary but it is done more as a business deal than a romantic proposition. So on the one hand we have had a scene in which Matthew and Mary say almost nothing to each other except goodbye and good luck, but we know and understand the deep love they feel for each other. And on the other, we have a proposal of marriage where love is hardly mentioned, let alone felt. (Although, when Sir Richard says later, after she has given him up, that he loved her – 'more than you knew' – one believes him completely.)

The station scenes are filmed at the Horstead Keynes station, one of four belonging to the Bluebell Railway, a heritage steam line in Sussex. Built in 1882 by the London Brighton and South Coast railway, it was originally a junction station. It has been restored by the Bluebell Railway to the 'Southern Railway' period, which is mid-1920s, with its distinctive green livery.

Quite a few of the larger country houses used to have their own station – one that sat on their estates. (Downton Station is in the village, rather than on the Abbey's land.) For some this was because they had invested in the railway, so this was a perk they had earned; others may have bargained for a station in return for handing over the land for the railway track. It was marvellously convenient for those that were lucky enough to have what amounted to a private train station. The Earl of Carlisle, in the late nineteenth century, was able to have fresh produce from his Yorkshire estate at Castle Howard on his table in Dublin the morning after it was picked. Even Rosamund can request saddles of lamb and fresh fruit and vegetables from the Home Farm – the family will put the produce on the train, cable Rosamund, and her butler will be sent to King's Cross to meet the parcels.

When the family visited Duneagle Castle, they all travelled by train.

With arrivals and departures the focus of a train station, it's natural that Julian should centre a dramatic storyline or two there. Not just the romantic kind, as we've seen with Mary. Carson was able to shake hands with Mr Grigg, his former music hall partner, after they made amends, thanks to Mrs Hughes's intervention. After Cora discovered the truth about Marigold, she persuaded Edith to return to Downton with her, where they would tell the story that the Drewes had decided they couldn't look after the little girl after all, so she was to become Edith's ward. They arranged to meet Drewe on the station as the three of them returned from London, to make it look as if he was handing Marigold over. Only their plan was almost scuppered when Mary and Anna were unexpectedly on the platform. In a flash, Drewe boarded the train and took Marigold alone onto the next stop, so that Cora and Edith could disembark. But Anna spotted the farmer and the little girl in the first class carriage as the train moved off and her suspicions were raised.

The grandest of people were never averse to travelling by train – Violet joined them all on the trip to Scotland. Of course, the family were in first class, their servants in third. But by 1925, travelling by train is no longer the most modern way to get around. Commercial airlines have begun to operate, and we hear the first hint of it in series six.

Flying to another country as a paying passenger must have seemed as exotic then as buying a ticket for a trip on a space shuttle to the moon does now. But perhaps we're not so far off that less than one hundred years later. In so many ways we are experiencing a parallel time with our forebears as we adjust to the exciting developments in technology all around us.

Matthew Crawley

DAN STEVENS

Matthew Crawley arrived at Downton Abbey as a young man who up to that point had led an upper-middle-class life as a lawyer, living with his widowed mother in Manchester. Bright, forward-thinking and good-looking, he was perfectly content with his life as it was. Receiving the news that he was the heir to an earldom in Yorkshire was not entirely welcome. He perceived that life to be one of stuffy formality, old-fashioned views, stifling tradition and, worst of all, the family were likely to push one of their three daughters at him to marry. Matthew arrived in 1912 and by the time war broke out two years later, he had been embraced by Robert as the son he'd never had, fallen in love with Mary and broken off their engagement, and become closely involved in the workings of the estate. Even Violet seemed to have become fond of this funny man who rode a bicycle and had a job. Away fighting, Matthew began to break his connections with the estate and even became engaged to another – Lavinia Swire. But a severe injury that left him believing he'd never walk again took him back to Downton and Mary was there, still in love with him, and willing to be his nurse. A sudden recovery took him out of the depression he was in and he and Lavinia planned to marry after all – even though he now realised he was still in love with Mary. But before the wedding could take place, Lavinia died of Spanish flu – Matthew believed it was really of a broken heart after she had seen him with Mary. Because of this he felt he could not marry Mary, nor could he take the money left to him by Lavinia's father, a fortune which could restore the losses Robert had made. Luckily, his mother persuaded him to see sense over Mary, and a letter from Lavinia was discovered that declared she wanted him only to be happy. Mary and Matthew married and after a while, she became pregnant. But on the day they welcomed their son, George, to the world, Matthew was killed in his car driving home.

Matthew and Mary as happy newlyweds looking forward to starting a family.

Matthew as he appeared over the three series, from lawyer to earl-in-waiting and soldier at war.

Isobel and her son Matthew arrive at their new home.

CRAWLEY HOUSE

MATTHEW AND ISOBEL CRAWLEY ARE BEING DRIVEN BY TAYLOR. THE CAR TURNS INTO A GATE.

TAYLOR: *Here we are, ma'am. Crawley House.*

MATTHEW: *For good or ill.*

Crawley House, part of the Downton estate and sitting within the village, was mustered for Isobel and Matthew Crawley, when they first arrived in 1912. The house is pretty, established and came with Molesley as butler and valet, as well as an extra maid, Beth. But it was an upheaval for the mother and son, who had to leave behind their work and social circle as part of Manchester's intellectual elite. Their previous townhouse had been narrow, modern and suited to their middle-class way of life – they had a cook, Mrs Bird, and a maid, Ellen, but otherwise looked after themselves and worked in any way they could.

It was deemed necessary for Matthew to live near Downton Abbey in order to get to know the house and estate well – and for those that lived there to get to know him – ahead of his inheritance. Matthew was never going to leave behind his widowed mother, as her only son, so she came, too. Isobel was punchy from the start, determined to make this drastic change of circumstance work for them and equally sure that she would not be patronised by the Crawleys. So she pluckily threw herself into village life, particularly when it came to the hospital, an area where she had confidence in her own knowledge and expertise. This meant that when her son died a few years later, Isobel was too embedded to leave – the family had adopted her, and she them. She decided to stay on at Crawley House.

Despite their increasing companionship, Isobel has a different outlook on life to Violet. Better educated than most women of the time, Isobel has worked as a nurse and enjoyed an atmosphere of medical learning both at home as a child and as the wife of a doctor. It is always Isobel who encourages the young to do things differently from before – whether it's Sybil training as a nurse to help the war effort or defending Branson's right to wear an ordinary suit at dinner. As set against Violet, who is equally certain in her own trenchant views, it makes for some colourful sparring between the two.

Isobel's more liberal viewpoint has meant that her house has been a refuge for those that needed her protection. Matthew, Mary and Branson (when he was still the chauffeur) took Sybil there after she was injured in the scuffle at the Ripon by-election. And when Isobel was away with the Red Cross in France, Mrs Bird and Molesley were bored with no work to do. When a former soldier came knocking on the door begging for some food, they decided to help and before long found there was a daily queue, all waiting for a handout of bread, fruit and stew. These walking wounded were a common sight during and after the war – men who were from the local area but no longer able to find work on a farm or in their previous field of employment. Mrs Bird and Molesley were soon helped by Mrs Patmore and Daisy, followed not long after by Cora, who insisted the food came from the house from then on.

Mrs Bird, Daisy and Mrs Patmore with food for the veterans.

Mrs Patmore tries to teach Ethel how to cook.

The rescue that was harder for some of the family to sympathise with was Ethel. Isobel met her in York, when she was working for the cause of 'fallen women'. Recognising that Ethel was a former housemaid of Downton Abbey, she became determined to help and soon roped Mrs Hughes in. Mrs Hughes was not a hard-hearted woman and she felt some element of guilt that Ethel's affair with Major Bryant had happened on her watch. Knowing that no one would employ such a girl, Isobel decided to take Ethel on herself. It was too much for those around her in 1921. Mrs Bird resigned, unable to work in a kitchen with a former prostitute. Carson forbade any of the servants to enter the house. And Ethel was increasingly treated shabbily by others in the village. It didn't really help matters that she was no good as a cook. Things came to a head when Isobel held a luncheon for Violet, Cora, Mary and Edith to show support for Cora, after the death of Sybil. Robert discovered that a streetwalker was serving his mother and wife, and stormed down to the house. Unfortunately, for him, they refused to budge.

More surprising than any of this for Isobel was the impassioned proposal by Lord Merton for her hand in marriage in her drawing room. This was a relationship she had resisted, despite Violet's teasing. She had been widowed for some years by then and enjoyed her simple life – minimal staff (she has never had a lady's maid) and a distinct lack of formality, as demonstrated by her preference when eating alone to sit in her drawing room, a tray upon her knees. But he wanted more than companionship – he declared freely that he had fallen in love. This was a harder entreaty to resist.

Sadly, it was broken by the furious sons, Timothy and Larry Grey. Isobel had no wish to be the cause of an estrangement between a man and his children, and she had little hesitation in calling it off. Perhaps because she had not felt the same as him, it was not too hard for her to do so but there's little doubt the idea of marriage to him had certainly appealed. There was a regret that lingered and when an explanation was proffered in the shape of the selfish Amelia Cruikshank, Larry's fiancée, she took it.

A simple house it may be relative to Downton Abbey, but Crawley House is in fact a composite of three different places. The exterior shots are filmed at Church Gate House, which is next to the church in Bampton, while the interiors are shot at Hall Place in Beaconsfield, excepting the kitchen, which is shot at Ham House in Surrey.

Occasionally, we glimpse the beautiful garden of Crawley House – the real-life owner is a keen gardener – and we see that Isobel enjoys doing some of her own pruning and weeding. Gardening in the 1920s was something that ladies were starting to do, alongside their gardeners, even if many had to contend with staff who did not particularly appreciate their contribution. Head gardeners of significant houses would often have worked for most of their careers outside, away from the family and with little interference; they became, therefore, rather defensive of their patch. Many's the mistress who wouldn't dare to pick a peach from the hothouse to eat on the walk back to the house, or choose some stems for a vase without express permission from her gardener. But after the war, as in the house, there were fewer men available to work in the gardens, and so partly out of necessity and partly because it was a pleasant way to fill one's time, more women went to work in their gardens – or at least, they liked to say that they did. Julian remembers even his own mother enjoying the 'Lady Bountiful' act by ensuring that she was walking up the path from the rose garden, basket full of freshly cut stems, just as guests arrived for lunch.

It was just by the garden gate that we saw the terribly sad scene in which Ethel handed her boy, Charlie, over to his grandparents, the Bryants. It was, of course, in order to give him the very best opportunities in life. Like his father, Charlie would receive a good education, be well supported financially (one wonders slightly about the emotional side of it) and probably be the heir to all Mr Bryant has. If mother and son had stayed together, life would have been a hard struggle. In time, the two may even be reunited – Ethel later took the chance to work close by so that she could see Charlie grow up and not lose contact with him.

The pretty Edwardian interior of Crawley House is not reflected in Isobel's dress. Free of her corset, she wears looser, more fashionable cuts, in very rich fabrics and bold prints. 'The dark colours, rich reds and dark silver really suit her,' says Anna Mary Scott Robbins, costume designer.

Crawley House turns out to be as charitable as its principal inhabitant, then, providing food for wounded soldiers and a refuge for Ethel. Isobel has made a success of her new life at Downton but she is a modern woman, one who embraces change and seeks improvement – as Violet remarked – with zeal. It was thanks to the likes of Isobel that the ways and traditions of old were not nearly as permanent as former generations had believed.

Ethel's emotional goodbye to her illegitimate son, Charlie, who was going to live with his grandparents, Mr and Mrs Bryant.

Mrs Reginald Crawley

PENELOPE WILTON

Penelope Wilton sits in the shade on a hot, bright day and talks with affection for her character about the qualities she admires in her: 'Her intelligence, her public-spiritedness and her loyalty. Also, she's a great one for looking ahead, she has been throughout – she fought the path for women's liberation, keen for them to have the vote and take their place on an equal footing with men, within the realm of her time.

'I understand her failings, too. She can be obsessive and bites off more than she can chew. She has opinions she has to live up to and she can meddle. But they all come from a good place. She's not petty.'

Penelope has wondered about Isobel's earlier life: 'Her back story, as Julian told it to me and as I have thought of it, is that she was married to a celebrated doctor who died at the time of the Boer War. Her father was also a celebrated, knighted doctor. She comes from a family of professionals. She herself has trained as a nurse, which would have been quite an advanced thing to do. She sees the rise of the professional classes and approves of it.'

This position of Isobel's gave her a good insight into the changes she saw happening around Downton Abbey: 'She reads, she notices things, she listens,' says Penelope.

Isobel is a dedicated, knowledgeable nurse.

Isobel wears elegant, simple shapes with rich colours and textiles.

ISOBEL

Aren't we the lucky ones?

'She is aware of the wider world. She is not the least resentful – or disapproving – of the Downton world. She is critical of the wider society and she wants to improve it. But she is not a radical socialist. Her desire to help is conceived within the existing structures of her world.'

Despite the fact that she has played the same character for so long, Penelope says that it doesn't change her as a person: 'I'm given dialogue to say and it's a mantle one assumes. It's an overcoat. I'm not like Isobel, she just comes through me.' One interesting point for the actors has always been that they don't get told what Julian has in store for their characters. So Penelope was delighted to find that in series six, Lord Merton was still in Isobel's life: 'One doesn't know – it was very interesting to find that he would come back and keep his flag flying. I don't mind not knowing, it's a bit like watching it – you live in the moment much more and you don't play the end, so you have to play exactly where you are.'

But it is Isobel's relationship with Violet that has been the most fun: 'They are sparring over pretty much everything. I've enjoyed that. They have also come to admire and be fond of one another, even need each other. They are opposites – they fall out and fall in all the time. They have moments when they don't see each other and then it all starts again. It's part of them. In real life (Maggie Smith) and I are very much more amicable!'

The differences between the two women are demonstrated through the way they dress too, with Isobel's clothes being much more relaxed and colourful. Of the costume designers, Penelope says admiringly, 'They've all been masters of what they do, I couldn't have had more help. I'm involved in as much as whether I like something and you know your own figure. But I'm in the hands of the most brilliant designer. The writer, the costume and make-up – the overall feeling has been wonderful right from the start. The framework within which we have worked has been so strong, it's been created for us. It's very easy to work in that world and hopefully bring out what Julian's been trying to achieve.'

Isobel embraces the modern trends of 1925.

Despite their sparring, Violet and Isobel have become friends.

Lord Merton
DOUGLAS REITH

Julian hadn't initially planned to bring Lord Merton back after the third series – he was first written in as the father of Larry Grey, a former suitor of Sybil's who was appallingly rude to Branson. After his appearance, Douglas Reith wrote to executive producer Liz Trubridge, to see if there might be any further storylines for him: 'I wrote in character, as Lord Merton,' laughs Douglas. 'I said that as I'm Mary's godfather, perhaps I ought to be seen again. And Liz wrote back to me "in character"!'

When he returned in the fourth series, he found himself cast as a suitor for Isobel Crawley, introduced to her by chance at Violet's house. On the face of it, Lord Merton and Isobel are not alike, and in their youth would have considered themselves as from very different social classes. But they share one particular thing, says Douglas: 'He's a member of his class without doubt but he's forward looking. Early on, he mentioned that as a peer he couldn't become a doctor. But he's not a stuffed shirt, he's not a snob.' Douglas likes his character: 'There's honesty about him, he's pragmatic. There's a slow boiling anger within but he's essentially a good man who had to cope with a difficult marriage.' Douglas enjoyed the romance between his character and Isobel. 'He sees her as a kindred spirit and a breath of fresh air. He played a subtle game, really, but I don't think he understood her not wanting to get between a father and son. Lord Merton struggled with Larry – he was so appalling and rude. It was difficult for him not to take his son outside and read the riot act!'

For all his modern views, the handsome Lord Merton is a man of his class.

With the woman he loves.

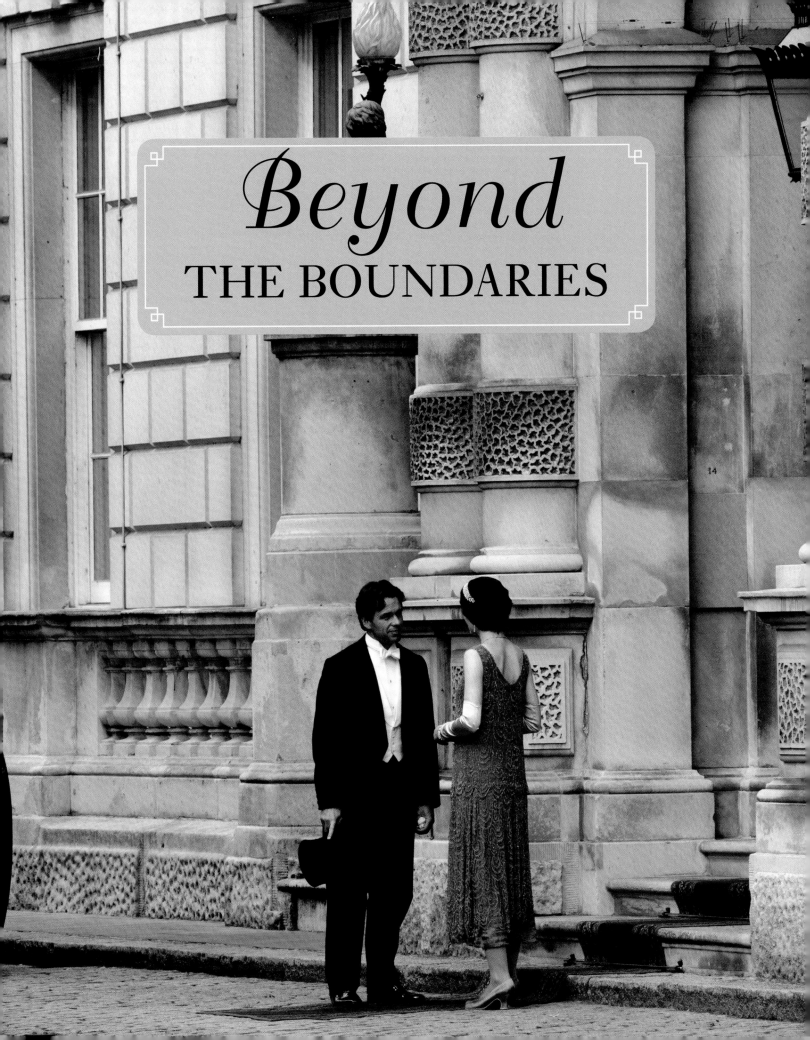

Beyond
THE BOUNDARIES

In the hallway of Rosamund's London house.

LONDON

MARY: *It's a funny thing about London, isn't it?*
The way it seems to draw one into
peculiar situations.

*I*n *Downton Abbey*, we watch the vast, sweeping changes of the early twentieth century take their effect on the house and its inhabitants – whether that be the adoption of labour-saving devices or women fighting for the right to vote. But part of the charm and comfort of the show is seeing how many of the house's residents resist that change, allowing it to alter their lives in small, incremental stages. Carson, Mrs Patmore, Violet and Robert want most of all to return things back to the way they were before the war; Mary, Edith, Cora and Mrs Hughes take the things from modern life that suit them; Tom, Rose, Daisy and Thomas are keen to take advantage of all that the new order can offer but often feel frustrated that they are still constrained by the old ways.

A hundred years before, in the 1820s, a place like Downton would, by and large, be the whole world for its inhabitants. Travel was slow and only a daily newspaper gave a window on the world beyond the estate. But in our Downton era, the family take the train to London often and with ease; there are newspapers, magazines, radio and the cinema all delivering images and (occasionally wild) ideas of how other lives are being lived. Life is, in short, less sheltered. The pace at Downton may move more slowly than elsewhere but in London it was going full-pelt and sometimes it was fun to be a part of it.

Robert's sister, Lady Rosamund Painswick, widow of the late Sir Marmaduke, has a splendid house in London that she seems happy to share with her brother and his family, whenever they need a bed for the night. The exterior for the house is filmed in London's Belgrave Square, but the interiors are from West Wycombe Park, the pretty Buckinghamshire home of Sir Edward Dashwood. Rosamund has money, thanks to her late husband, and with no children of her own, is closely involved with her nieces. She is of Robert's generation, so although she may wear more fashionable clothes than her sister-in-law, her views are not always progressive.

BRANSON

People don't want vast palaces any more, even if they can afford them.

ROBERT

They were fun, though. In my youth, all the great hostesses used to have luncheon laid for twenty every day and if you turned up in time, you just sat down to a lovely feed.

When she discovered that Edith had come back to the house in the early hours of the morning, having been to dine with Michael Gregson, she warned her niece that this was dangerous behaviour.

Despite the fact that the family stay with Rosamund when in town for a night or two, they have their own house. Grantham House is the London palace for the Crawleys but, in common with many such buildings owned by the great families, it was chiefly designed for hosting large parties during the season. While they pay for a housekeeper – Mrs Bute – to live there full-time until 1925, opening up a house to stay would have been considered more trouble than it was worth. There were large state rooms, ideal for balls, but sleeping accommodations were typically smaller than those of their country houses. Of course, this impracticality meant that the London houses were the first to go when families started to run out of money. Even those who could still afford them felt they belonged to a life that no longer existed. In that, at least, they were right.

In the summer of 1923, almost the entire Downton household decamped to London for Rose's coming-out ball. The debutante season marked the moment a girl left the schoolroom and entered the ballroom. While the young men and women enjoyed the chance at last to behave as grown-ups, with dances, parties, luncheons and afternoon teas, all within the London season, it had chiefly operated for some time as a well-orchestrated marriage market. The aristocracy came together with their children in the hopes that they would then meet and fall in love with 'the right sort' of bride or groom. Rose's generation, the post-war youth that didn't really remember life before, were less apt to seek their husbands seriously in this whirlwind, but they certainly enjoyed the dresses and the parties.

For the rest of the family, it was a chance to see their old friends as everyone gathered in the capital. Grantham House was opened up and in the final episode of the fourth series, we saw most of Downton Abbey's servants join them, too. Not that it was necessarily very exciting for them – as Daisy remarked, peeling potatoes in London was much the same as peeling them in Yorkshire.

Martha and Harold Levinson had come to enjoy the season, too (perhaps rather more reluctantly on Harold's part), and soon found themselves targeted as marriage material as much as a pair of pretty debs, thanks to their enormous riches. But the two of them were wise to any ruse and quite easily batted off Lord Aysgarth and his daughter, Madeleine.

ROSE

Hmm, we're packed in like sardines,
but I suppose it's not for long.

MRS PATMORE

If the family's sardines, m'lady,
the staff are like maggots.

Almost the whole household relocated to Grantham House
for Lady Rose's wedding to Atticus Aldridge, which required
additional help in the form of footman, Andy.

During his visit to London, Harold Levinson found himself pursued by a fortune hunter, Madeleine Allsopp.

The exterior of Grantham House was filmed at Cleveland Row in London but the interiors are Basildon Park in Berkshire, a National Trust property. (The picnic scene that supposedly took place in Hyde Park was filmed in the grounds here, too.) The impressive staircase that opens out into the hall, and the Octagon Room with its rich red walls, used as the family's drawing room when they host Rose and Atticus's engagement party at the end of the fifth series, can be seen here. The house's dining room was seen as the ballroom for the climax of the final episode of season four, when Rose had her coming-out ball and the Prince of Wales asked her for the first dance.

When Rose's presentation at Buckingham Palace was filmed in London it happened to coincide with the impending birth of Prince George to the Duke and Duchess of Cambridge, which meant, as Liz Trubridge recalled, that a great many roads they hoped to go down were blocked off! Filming in London is always a challenge: partly because any shoot in a public place threatens to be swamped by fans and partly because the practicality of parking the very big unit of Downton Abbey is both expensive and a logistical horror.

The interiors for Buckingham Palace were shot at Goldsmiths Hall and Lancaster House but other places were filmed exactly where they were set. Rules restaurant, the Criterion Restaurant and the Embassy nightclub were all fitting locations given that they have changed little in the last hundred years. These places were settings for liaisons between Mary or Edith and their beaux, or as the backdrop for the flappers and Bright Young Things that Rose surrounded herself with. The point about London was that it was somewhere the girls, particularly, could feel freer from the inhibitions and rules that governed their lives at home. As they moved into the 1920s, certain conventions from before the war were dropped, and of course they themselves were older and less accountable to their parents. At last, they could go out without chaperones, go to nightclubs and meet some of the more interesting, even Bohemian, people of the time.

In the final series, Edith is in London a great deal, overseeing the change of editorship of the magazine she has inherited from Michael Gregson. Edith's magazine, *The Sketch*, was a popular publication of the time, published by the Illustrated London News Company from 1893 to 1959. It happened to be the first magazine to publish short stories by Agatha Christie. Initially, scenes set in the office were filmed in a very expensive and sought-after location in East London. Three days were spent setting it up, even though its first appearance – in the third series – was just one scene long. It was deemed worth it because it was a great way

Tom, Edith, and Mary join Rose for lunch at Rules, shortly before she marries Atticus.

ROSAMUND

Oh my dear, how exotic. I expect to find the whole of the Bloomsbury Set curled up in a corner with a book.

EDITH

Michael knew quite a few of them, actually. I met Virginia Woolf in this room and Lytton Strachey, in fact, although he didn't stay very long.

Edith with Michael Gregson in his London flat, which became her very own bolt-hole in the sixth series.

Edith confronts her editor, Mr Skinner, in *The Sketch* office.

to illustrate just how different life was in London from Downton Abbey, with women working in the office, typing and smoking and so on.

For series six, so many more scenes were written in the office that it made more practical sense to recreate it in the studios. Linda Wilson, the set dresser, particularly enjoyed this as it tells the story of Edith in a completely different way. The biggest challenge for Linda was having the layout pages for the magazine created.

In series six, we also saw more of Edith's London flat (which she had also inherited from Michael Gregson). Again, while this was initially filmed on location in a beautiful apartment in Notting Hill, logistics made it more sensible to build it as a set in the studios for the later shoots. The flat tells the tale of Michael Gregson's life as one that is different to Edith's – he was middle-class, yes, but more importantly he was part of London's alternative scene – filled with the famous writers and artists of the time.

This, too, reveals another side to Edith – we understand that she fitted in with these people, was possibly found to be amusing and fun to be with. At home, we have seen Edith as sometimes rather narrow-minded and mean but London – and life – have changed her. Rather than being fed up with her lot, Edith decides to take control, with the result that she becomes a much more attractive and nice person to be with.

In London, Edith has confidence away from her family, and her work with the magazine, which she comes to derive great satisfaction from. While she seems increasingly to find London the place that brings out the best in her, Mary has remained ambivalent. It is the place for shopping, fashion and catching up with one's friends; and it is in the city, away from the usual expectations and pressures of the estate, that Mary feels able to embark on a bold flirtation. She enjoys the click of her heels on the pavement, as she has said, but when she is in London she always yearns for the country; for Mary, it is not the place to live.

The Crawleys and MacClares gather at Grantham House, shortly after Rose's engagement to Atticus is announced. This interior was filmed on location at Basildon Park – note the lighting and microphone.

VIOLET

So Lady Rose MacClare is a mésalliance?

EDITH

I'm not sure that's helpful, Granny.

Lady Rosamund Painswick

SAMANTHA BOND

The older sister of Robert, Rosamund lives in London in the house she inherited from her late husband, Sir Marmaduke Painswick. 'I think it was a happy marriage,' says Samantha Bond. 'She grew up knowing the son gets everything, so she made a clever marriage to a much older man. Now she has her beautiful house, she has money, she has clothes – she's a merry widow.' They had no children, so she is close to her nieces and appears to enjoy having the family to stay with her when they need a day or two in the city. (In fact, in the show's original press release, Rosamund was given two children as part of her back story, but Julian decided it would be more interesting if she was shown living her life vicariously through her nieces.) Rich and living in the capital, Rosamund is more fashionable than Cora, which gives the costume department licence to do even more thrilling outfits. 'I win in the hat department,' says Samantha. 'Especially this one even though it is murder. I daren't take it off for the feeling of relief and have to put it back on again.'

Hard-headed and snobbish, Rosamund's ambition outpaces even that of her own mother and Mary. When Cora was pregnant and it looked as if Matthew might be displaced as heir she advised Mary not to accept his marriage proposal straight away, which even Violet thought was a terrible idea. When Matthew later turned up with Lavinia Swire as his fiancée, Rosamund failed to sympathise with Mary. 'Why must she be so savage?' says Mary, in one of her few vulnerable moments. 'It's her fault my heart is broken.'

When, ostensibly in her care in London, Edith spent the night with Michael Gregson, Rosamund was quick to remind her that she had taken a huge risk. She revealed herself to be worldly – 'please don't tell me you stayed up all night talking and lost track of time' – and less concerned with the (absence of) morals than Edith's trusting her reputation to a man she was not married to: 'You're gambling with your future, my dear. Be under no illusions. A lot may be changing but some things will stay the same.' Nonetheless, she agreed to keep Edith's secret and when her niece told her she was pregnant, it was Rosamund who not only provided her with a way out but accompanied her for several months to Switzerland so that she could have her child safely before handing her over to another family.

Rosamund hasn't a sentimental hair on her head and is a woman of her class and time. But she is like her mother in one important respect: family comes first. 'She has many admirable qualities,' says Samantha. 'I feel very close to her. She's an honourable woman.'

Rosamund often accompanies her nieces to events in London.

Rosamund's wardrobe features a lot of vintage pieces. Her signature palette is autumnal, and dramatic hats are a key part of her look.

Mrs Isidore Levinson

SHIRLEY MacLAINE

Cora's mother, Martha Levinson, arrived at the start of the third series and her entrance was far from quiet. It was very deliberate, of course. Martha may have been a grandmother, but she was modern and represented the rich, confident American that looked forward, not back.

In short, Martha was in direct contrast to Violet. This is particularly evident if you look at their costumes. Where Violet still wore the style dictated by Queen Mary, with her high-necked collars, S-bend corset and Edwardian lace trimmings, Martha embraced the post-war fashion. They were not friends and clashed openly over their difference of attitude. It was key, therefore, that the production cast an actress who could match Maggie Smith for on-screen weight. They wanted Shirley MacLaine and to their delight, she accepted. Executive producer Liz Trubridge says the memory of the two actresses working together will stay with her for a long time.

The intention at first was to have Martha appear in just the first few episodes of the third series but she proved such a hit that she was brought back, alongside her son, Harold (played by Paul Giamatti), for the final episode of the fourth series, in which Rose had her debutante season. She may not have been a great support to her daughter, a bully to her granddaughters and Violet's foe but she was hugely entertaining. Doubtless she returned to America and her many houses to continue her comfortable, happy life.

In the fourth series Martha returned to England with her playboy son, Harold.

Martha enjoys displaying her riches in her clothes and jewels.

Mary is proud of her pigs.

YORKSHIRE

EXT. THE MALTON FAT STOCK SHOW. DAY.

This is a modest, muddy show, in an open square, with the emphasis on fattened livestock. But there are some stalls and simple shies of games and produce, while the animals are paraded and judged in different fenced arenas.

*I*t's no accident that *Downton Abbey* is set in Yorkshire. Julian went to school there, at Ampleforth, and as his parents were largely abroad, he was home only three times a year. In short, Yorkshire was where Julian spent his teenage years and he has remained fond of it ever since – the wild moors, the soft stone of its architecture, the accents of its inhabitants. And although Julian always had Highclere Castle in mind as the perfect location for the show, executive producer Gareth Neame and production designer Donal Woods looked at many houses in Yorkshire in case the right one was there, before deciding on Highclere, which is in Berkshire.

Downton Abbey is, of course, fictional, as is its village. The name is borrowed from Downton Agricultural College, which was founded by Julian's great-grandfather, John Wrightson (The Wrightsons descended from Eryholme in Yorkshire, which was the name Julian gave to the smaller house the Crawleys almost had to move into). But the places that the characters often travel to are quite real – York, Ripon, Thirsk, Malton, Haughton-le-Skerne. As with so much else Downton, there's often a blur between where reality ends and fiction begins – the stories told are all things that very well might have happened, had those people lived there at that time. Real-life backdrops underline this.

Ripon is a beautiful old market town, founded over 1,300 years ago. A site for monasteries, it was the obvious choice for Sybbie's Catholic christening. It's only nine miles from Downton – but would have more to offer than the village in terms of shops and even a theatre (Jimmy takes Ivy to see the Dare Sisters) without having to go as far as York. Lady Rose asks Anna to accompany her to a thé dansant for farmers and servants in Ripon – although it was actually filmed in Hoxton Hall in London.

Ripon is the setting for Matthew's office, the solicitor's firm, Harvell & Carter. To get there he bicycled to Downton Station from Crawley House, then hopped on a train. Anna and Bates married in the register office here – there wouldn't have been one in the village, so it was necessary for them to travel a bit further.

Most dramatically, Ripon was the setting for the political rallies that Sybil attended in May 1914. In Ripon Market Place, a crowd assembled beneath the windows of the town hall for the by-election results. There was fury at the defeat of the Liberals and fights broke out – Sybil was knocked out in the fracas.

Six miles in the other direction to Ripon, marginally closer to Downton, is Thirsk, another market town, which was perhaps a little more convenient. It's here that Tom met Sarah Bunting at the town hall, where he went, with Isobel's encouragement, to hear MP John Ward give a talk. It's also where Tom spotted Lady Rose having tea with the jazz singer, Jack Ross, which led to Mary calling time on their affair. Thirsk was the setting for the Netherby Hotel, where Anna and Bates went for a rare night out, only to be treated shabbily by the maitre d' – he was soon forced to eat his hat, after Cora intervened. Thirsk Fair, where Mrs Patmore was taken by Joe Tufton, was filmed at Eton College. At the same fair, Dr Clarkson almost proposed to Isobel Crawley, and Thomas was beaten up after intervening in a fight between Jimmy and local thugs.

As Anna is recovering from her ordeal, Bates takes her to a restaurant at the Netherby Hotel in Thirsk, where Cora rescues them from a snooty maître d'.

All the fun of the fair for Alfred, Ivy, Daisy, Jimmy, Tom and Thomas, in the final episode of the third series.

The town of Malton was the setting for the Fat Stock Show: with Mr Mason joining the servants, Mary winning a prize for her pigs and the Crawleys enjoying a family day out.

Mrs Patmore takes Mrs Hughes to see her new bed and breakfast.

The town of Malton makes a brief appearance in the final series as the setting for the Fat Stock Show. This annual event still takes place in some old market towns – it's for show and sell, with the emphasis on fattened livestock. But the general atmosphere is one of friendly muddiness, with stalls for produce and simple games, as the animals are paraded and judged in different fenced areas. The scenes were filmed at Lacock in Wiltshire, an unspoilt village mostly owned by the National Trust.

Venturing out into the wide world, or at least the county of Yorkshire, is Mrs Patmore. With the money she had inherited, she invested in a cottage to run as a bed and breakfast to earn her a little income and provide her with somewhere to live on retirement. Without this, Mrs Patmore would have nothing but the small savings she may have been able to accumulate.

Also in the county of Yorkshire is the Red Lion pub of Kirkbymoorside, where Bates went to work in series two. Eventually, Robert and Anna traced him here and persuaded him to return. The pub is actually the Old Forge in Shilton, a few miles north-west of Bampton. It sits alongside the Shill Brook and we also caught a glimpse of the pretty eighteenth-century stone hump-backed bridge that sits across the river there.

Ancient and handsome York is the closest city to Downton Abbey. Although the family tends to go to London if there's anything they need that only a city can provide – whether department stores, doctors or the click of heels on the pavement – York

In the York courthouse, Mary watches as Anna and Bates react to his death sentence.

has still featured in the Downton sphere. Sybil went there to train at the College of Nursing, during the war. Rose found a cause in the city – looking after Russian refugees, by giving them tea and cake every Tuesday and Thursday in the crypt of a church, the Chapel of St Mary Magdalene. (And it was thanks to buying those cakes, one rainy day, that she bumped into her future husband, Atticus Aldridge.) After the war, Isobel had her cause there, too, rescuing 'fallen women', which was when she came across former housemaid Ethel, forced to turn to prostitution to feed herself and her son Charlie. It was also the sad scene of Mrs Hughes's discovery of Mr Grigg in the workhouse.

But it was York Prison that had the starring role in the show. The prison has housed both Bates and Anna. Bates was sentenced to death at trial, pronounced guilty of murdering his wife, Vera. After Anna had found the evidence to commute his sentence to life imprisonment and then, finally, to acquit him altogether, Bates was freed.

This meant Bates spent most of the third series in prison, which was a rather isolating time for the actor, Brendan Coyle, as his scenes were filmed on location – in the Old Crown Court at Kingston for the court room and the prison waiting room, at Lincoln Castle's Victorian prison for the exterior shots and the prison courtyard, and at Chalfont Campus for the prison itself. 'The prison where we filmed was extraordinary, it had great drama and scope. It's a museum, perfectly preserved. When we were walking along the [internal] bridges, you could hear the doors slamming behind you. I remember the cells vividly, too. You could see how brutal the regime was and what hard labour they did. It was unusual being away from the cast I usually work with but then because there are so many of us, it's rare we're all in on the same day. Quite often it's just me and Jo [Froggatt].'

Whilst shopping for cakes in the famous Bettys tea rooms in York, Rose meets Atticus Aldridge for the first time.

Duneagle Castle in Scotland plays host to the Crawleys.

GREAT ESTATES

This is a fairytale castle, with turrets and battlements and secret windows. The family party climbs out of two cars as Shrimpie, his wife, Susan, and Rose greet them.

When going to other big houses, the challenge for location manager Mark Ellis was to find places that were dramatically different and distinct from Downton, whilst also reflecting the time and characters involved.

The aristocracy did not take 'holidays' as we know them today until the second half of the twentieth century. Without jobs to tie them down or even school term dates to worry about (children would either be taught by their governess or staying at boarding school), they were free to go somewhere whenever they wanted. Nor did they stay in hotels but always with friends or relations. Ladies' maids and valets travelled with them and possibly their chauffeur too if they drove the whole way (though travelling by train was more usual for longer distances). Before trains, going to stay with someone could take several days and it would not be unusual to remain there for weeks at a time. With the advent of trains and motorcars, the 'Saturday-to-Monday' house party became the norm. The 'weekend', which mischievous Violet made such play with, was a modern concept adopted by the middle classes who both had a job and jumped in their car to stay with friends in the country from Friday to Sunday.

House parties often centred around the sporting seasons – shoots in the late nineteenth century and onwards were particularly popular, thanks to the influence of Kings Edward VII and George V who were mad about the sport. Staying in order to join a hunt was less usual but certainly a reasonable enough excuse. Many great houses were centres of political power, which ensured a certain amount of angling for an invitation. When staff were plentiful, there were up to fifty guest bedrooms and the estate could provide a surplus of meat and vegetables, having people to stay was not considered an outrageous expense – it was part of the reason your house existed at all.

Inveraray Castle (pronounced 'Inverara') in the West Highlands is the real-life setting for Lady Rose's childhood home, Duneagle Castle, estate of the Marquess of Flintshire. The idea to use it came from historical advisor Alastair Bruce, who knows the owners, the Duke and Duchess of Argyll – they had said that should Downton ever want to go to Scotland, they'd love their house to be used. Alastair mentioned it to Julian and so it happened! It is a fabulously romantic Scottish castle with turrets and towers, built to a design by the famous eighteenth-century architects Robert Morris and William Adam – it took forty years to complete after the first foundation stone was laid and was finished by Adam's two sons.

Alnwick Castle is the real-life Brancaster Castle, seen in the final episode of the fifth season as the grand estate rented by Lord Sinderby for a shooting party. When the cast and crew decamped there it was the longest they had ever spent away from their usual homes of Highclere and Ealing Studios, which created something of a holiday atmosphere (albeit one in which the alarm calls were rather earlier than you might enjoy *en vacances*). In all they were filming at the castle and in its grounds and parklands for two weeks during the summer of 2014.

Belonging to the Duke of Northumberland, it has been in his family for more than 700 years. The state rooms are perfectly preserved and lent themselves brilliantly to the show but there were some challenges involved. Producer Chris Croucher recalls that lighting the drawing room meant building scaffolding on the outside that went two floors up.

We have also seen brief glimpses of other stately homes. Set on the edge of the Vale of the White Horse in Wiltshire, the handsome Kingston Bagpuize House is used as Cavenham Park, Lord Merton's house, where we saw Isobel and Violet have lunch with him. Later it was also the scene of Violet's and then Isobel's confrontations with his future daughter-in-law, Amelia, over her desire to see him married off (she didn't want to be his nurse). Hall Barn Estate in Beaconsfield plays the role of the handsome home Edith expected to be moving into with Sir Anthony Strallan. This house was also used as Lady Trentham's (played by Maggie Smith) in the opening shot of *Gosford Park*. And Waddesdon Manor was used for Haxby Hall, the house that Sir Richard Carlisle intended would be a home for him and Mary. When they broke up, he stayed true to form by telling her not to worry about the house – he would be selling it on at a profit.

Grey's Court in Henley was the setting for Eryholme, the smaller house belonging to the Downton estate that the family thought they might have to move to when Robert lost all the money in a bad investment. Julian was keen for a while on this move – it would have reflected well the change that many families of the time had to make – but it was felt in the end that the original house was too integral a part of the show. Instead we saw them have a picnic on the lawn without going into the house – which was being rented by tenants – but we saw enough to see that, as Cora remarked, while it was smaller than Downton, a move to Eryholme was hardly the same as having to go down the mines.

When Robert feared he would lose Downton Abbey, he considered a move to Eryholme, a smaller house he owned further north, and so took the family there for a picnic.

Alnwick Castle is the location used for Brancaster Castle. Tea and cake in the splendid drawing room; later Mary dances with guest Henry Talbot.

Lady Rose MacClare

LILY JAMES

Rose was Downton's wild child: young, lively, and the one who couldn't remember life before the war, so had no nostalgia for that period. Instead, she embraced the youth, fashion and brave new world of post-war Britain and America. Stifled by her mother Susan and made unhappy by her parents' constant bickering, she came to live with Robert and Cora in the fourth series. 'They became her surrogate parents and she owes a lot to them,' says Lily James. 'They saved her from her mother at a time when she was going down the wrong path.' Violet was also keen that Rose did not join Lord and Lady Flintshire in India, where she would be sure to marry a 'third-rate colonial official with no money and bad teeth'.

Cora was only too delighted to welcome her in and treated her like one of her daughters, even hosting her splendid debutante season – the first year in which things had returned to form after the First World War enforced a hiatus. Pretty, mischievous and just rebellious enough, Rose knew how to enjoy herself. She enlisted Anna's help in getting her to a local dance for farmers and servants, posing as a maid from Downton Abbey – and almost getting caught out when a 'gentleman caller' came knocking on the back door. Later, she fell for the handsome, dashing bandleader Jack Ross – he also happened to be black, which in 1923 was a liberalism too far even for the Crawleys. (Ross was based on a black jazz musician, Hutch, who was famed for his affairs with high society women in London in the 1920s.)

Slightly stuck for something to do, Rose took up the cause of the Russian refugees – aristocrats who had fled from the Revolution – taking them cake and asking them all about their lives. As she freely admitted, life for her was dancing and seeing her friends. It was as she came out of the cake shop in York one rainy day that she bumped into Atticus Aldridge, the handsome young man who quickly became her husband – once they had overcome the hurdle of her gentile background and Susan and Shrimpie's impending divorce, both of which caused her Jewish father-in-law initial displeasure. In the sixth season, Rose was heard of again as living in New York, happily married and enjoying the high life. 'She's incredibly loyal but also astute,' says Lily. 'She cares for those that have taken care of her and is not afraid to meddle and get stuck in. Over the years, it's been a lovely development with her, having gone from a fickle merry-maker with no regard for others' feelings to being caring and generous. She's channelled that energy into becoming a strong woman.'

Rose's wardrobe shifted to reflect her growing up, but it was always fun and youthful.

Rose in her wedding dress for the blessing of her marriage to Atticus.

Mrs Patmore enjoys a day at the seaside.

HIGH DAYS & HOLIDAYS

MRS HUGHES: *We ought to have the outing settled if we're going on Thursday.*

CARSON: *Oh? I feel a little guilty about that. I tried out my ideas on them and I couldn't fire up any enthusiasm, so I wonder if we should just settle for a day by the sea.*

Every series of *Downton Abbey* features a set piece which sees the family and servants do something different from their usual routine and also celebrates a quintessentially British pastime – picnics, fairs, cricket, a trip to the seaside, a point-to-point, a garden party, a car race. Filming these always takes place on location, which means a big change for cast and crew too as everybody relocates for a few days. Logistically it requires immensely careful planning – parking the huge mobile trucks that house the costume, hair and make-up and production offices, the catering trucks, the many cars; the hotel accommodation that has to be booked. Not to mention finding the location and ensuring that all the equipment that will be needed will be there on the day. Filming on location also often involves hiring extras for crowds or people walking in the background – each one has to be cast, then fitted for a costume, as well as dressed and made up on the day.

Some of the locations used were not entirely obvious – when the servants had their much-deserved day off by the sea at the end of a few long weeks in London, West Wittering beach was used as Brighton beach. This was the moment Ethan, Harold Levinson's valet, tried to persuade Daisy to join him in America as his girlfriend and Harold's cook. She said no but was delighted by the proposal – Ivy took the opportunity instead, to be the cook, at least! And it was here we watched the fourth series finish with Carson and Mrs Hughes paddling into the sea together, hand in hand. A happy note and a sign of things to come, as it turned out.

The setting for Brooklands, a famous racetrack in the 1920s, was Goodwood, which is home every year to a revival race, so already has the authentic vintage look needed. Filmed over three days, 210 extras were hired for the crowds, which meant very early call times, in order to get everyone dressed and ready for the start of filming. From six o'clock there were long queues for costume, hair and make-

MARY

But what's the point?
What do they get out of it?

BRANSON

What do you think? Speed!

The car race at Brooklands proved to be an eventful day for the Crawley family and their servants.

Mary chose the point-to-point to debut her shocking new bobbed haircut, stealing the thunder from her old love-rival Mabel Lane Fox.

up, and breakfast! Each extra was cast as either working class or upper class and a great many were mechanics and drivers (they had black stuff rubbed into their hands, under their fingernails and on their cheeks, to look like smears of oil). The men surprisingly had a long queue for hair and make-up, as each one had his hair slicked down with old-fashioned pomade. Several men were asked to shave their non-period beards, while others had moustaches carefully stuck on.

For filming itself, the crowds were managed by the first and second assistant directors. Extras would pair up or be put into small groups and given a small storyline or instruction that would keep them focused during filming – to chat for a few minutes, then on a given cue walk across to a different spot, wait for another extra to come along and then walk elsewhere and so on. Or extras would be asked to walk at a certain time across the background of two of the main cast filming dialogue.

The director for the episode, David Evans, used the film *Rush* (about racing drivers James Hunt and Niki Lauda) for inspiration. He counted seventy-five shots used in a ninety-second race sequence which he sought to replicate almost exactly. But even he was amazed at the amount of work that went into getting the race crowds filmed. 'I've never worked with so many backstage cameras. It does make you quite self-conscious,' he laughs.

The shoot took place in mid-June, out of sequence with the rest of the series – the race happens in episode eight, though they were still filming episode five at the time – but it was the only time the racetrack was free so had to be done then. The sun shone brightly and the extras were soon sweltering under their wigs and hats, not to mention layers of stockings, slips or a double-breasted suit and waistcoat.

Nonetheless, the excitement of being part of the show, even if one is only glimpsed for a second or two in the final edit, is enough to withstand the heat and long hours on one's feet. I must declare a bias as I was one of the extras for this episode and it was tremendous indeed to see it all from the other side of the camera.

When one thinks of *Downton Abbey*, one thinks of the great house as the centre of the show, almost a character in its own right. But I hope you have seen here that there was more to the family and their servants than the one roof they lived under. An estate such as Downton Abbey held land and sway far beyond its own walls. It's a way of life that no longer exists in Britain but the best of it may still be celebrated in our historical houses, our ancestral memories and, dare I say it, as we sit comfortably on our sofas and watch the show again.

EPISODE GUIDE

SERIES ONE

Episode One ▼

Directed by: **Brian Percival**
Written by: **Julian Fellowes**

We begin with John Bates on the train, on his way to become valet to the Earl of Grantham, with whom he worked during the Boer War. A telegram arrives announcing the deaths of Patrick and James Crawley on the *Titanic*. Patrick was Robert's heir and his eldest daughter, Lady Mary's, fiancé. Robert's American wife Lady Grantham's money is tied up in the entail – can this be smashed so that Mary may become sole heiress to the estate and her mother's, fortune, if not the title? The Duke of Crowborough comes to stay but he is a fortune hunter and will not be asking Mary to marry him. It is revealed that the duke had an affair with Thomas, the first footman. Robert decides he will not fight the entail but will write to the heir. The servants complain that Bates's limp prevents him from working properly. Robert dismisses him but has a change of heart at the last minute.

Episode Two ▲
Directed by: **Ben Bolt**
Written by: **Julian Fellowes**

Matthew, the heir, and his mother, Isobel, arrive at Downton to live at Crawley House. Isobel wishes to work with the local hospital; Violet, the Dowager Countess, is outraged at the idea. Matthew reveals that he will continue to work as a solicitor with a local firm, which Robert cannot understand. After he is seen smuggling food from the larder, it's revealed that the butler, Carson, used to be a music hall act with Mr Grigg, who blackmails him. The housemaid, Gwen, has a secret correspondence. The second footman William Mason has a crush on Daisy the kitchen maid but she is in love with Thomas. Isobel interferes in a treatment for a local farmer, John Drake, who has dropsy. Mary reveals she has an impressive suitor: the Hon. Evelyn Napier.

Episode Three ▼
Directed by: **Ben Bolt**
Written by: **Julian Fellowes**

Fellow housemaid Anna discovers Gwen's secret – she wants to be a secretary. Cora suggests that Mary invite Evelyn and a Turkish diplomat to stay while they are nearby to ride with the hunt. Mary is overcome when she meets Kemal Pamuk. Bates buys a painful contraption in an attempt to cure his limp; Mrs Hughes discovers it and makes him throw it away. Lady Edith, Lord Grantham's middle daughter, makes a play for Matthew, inviting him to visit local churches. Pamuk goes to Mary's room at night and dies suddenly. She is forced to ask Anna and her mother for help to drag him back to his room; they are spotted by Daisy. Thomas tells O'Brien, Cora's lady's maid, that he took Pamuk to Mary's room; he does not reveal that he made a pass at him, which was turned down in no uncertain terms.

Episode Four ▲
Directed by: **Brian Kelly**
Written by: **Julian Fellowes and Shelagh Stephenson**

Downton Fair has come to the village. The new chauffeur arrives – Tom Branson. He has an interest in history and politics. Isobel inspects the red raw marks on her butler Molesley's hands; she suggests he may have to wear gloves – but he says he can't, he'd look like a footman. Anna has a cold. Violet goes to see Matthew to ask if he can be sure of the exact terms of his inheritance. Joe Burns comes to the fair to see housekeeper Elsie Hughes, his former sweetheart. Matthew goes to see Robert about the entail. Bates takes supper up to the sick Anna, with flowers in a vase. Thomas takes Daisy to the fair just to get at William but raises false hopes for her. Mary realises that she will never be the heiress – she and Matthew have a lingering handshake. Bates threatens Thomas, showing his angry side – Thomas claims it's 'not working'. Lady Sybil, the youngest daughter, persuades Gwen to take a sick day so that she can go to an interview. Branson drives Sybil to the dressmaker – he tells her he is interested in politics and gives her some pamphlets. Robert and Matthew go to see the old tenants' cottages.

Episode Five ▼
Directed by: Brian Kelly
Written by: Julian Fellowes

Daisy has flashbacks of seeing Pamuk's body being carried into a guest room. Sybil has applied for another job as secretary for Gwen. Bates spots Thomas stealing a bottle of wine from the cellar. Robert has heard that Evelyn Napier has given up on Mary – there's a suggestion that Mary has been found wanting in her character. Isobel gets involved in the Downton Flower Show, especially once she hears that Violet always wins. One of Robert's snuffboxes goes missing; Bates has been set up by Thomas and O'Brien but gets his own back. Mrs Patmore, the cook, refuses to cook a new recipe for Cora. Sir Anthony Strallan is invited to dinner as a potential suitor for Mary but she finds him dull. At the dinner, Mrs Patmore puts salt instead of sugar on the meringues; she tearfully admits to Carson she is going blind. O'Brien tells Edith that Daisy knows something about Mary and Pamuk. In revenge for Mary making a sudden play for Strallan, Edith writes to the Turkish Ambassador. Anna tells Bates she loves him. Violet decides to award the prize for best roses to Bill Molesley.

Episode Six ▲
Directed by: Brian Percival
Written by: Julian Fellowes and Tina Pepler

May 1914. Sybil attends the Ripon by-election; Branson finds her and gets her away. Dr Clarkson, the family doctor, confirms Mrs Patmore has cataracts. Carson hears from a friend about Mary and Pamuk and tells Cora. Bates is accused of stealing wine by Thomas and O'Brien – they persuade Daisy to lie and say she saw him coming out of the cellar. Cora is forced to admit to Violet that the story she has heard about Mary is true. William's mother has a fatal heart illness and is dying but doesn't want him to know. Strallan asks Edith to a concert. Sybil goes to the results of the vote at Ripon and is caught up in the fight; she is injured. Branson and Matthew take her back to Crawley House and fetch Mary. Bates is found innocent of the stealing after Daisy admits to lying; but then he reveals he was a drunkard and a thief in the past. Mary and Matthew are alone in the dining room and admit to feelings for each other; they kiss and he proposes.

Episode Seven ▲
Directed by: Brian Percival
Written by: Julian Fellowes

July 1914. Cora discovers she is pregnant – Robert is delighted. Violet's lady's maid is leaving; Cora offers to help her find another one by placing an ad in *The Lady*. O'Brien overhears and thinks she is being dismissed; she is furious. She punishes Cora by leaving half a bar of soap on the floor by her bath – Cora slips on it and loses the baby. They discover it would have been a boy. Mary has not accepted Matthew's proposal quickly enough. He thinks she is delaying because she is not sure whether or not he will be the heir and calls it off. At the garden party Mary avenges herself on Edith by telling Strallan that Edith had been complaining about a frightful old bore – he decides not to propose after all. Robert comes into the garden and reads a telegram that announces the start of the war.

SERIES TWO

Episode One ▼
Directed by: **Ashley Pearce**
Written by: **Julian Fellowes**

November 1916, during the Battle of the Somme. Matthew returns home from the front, with his fiancée Lavinia Swire. At Downton Abbey they hold a fundraising concert for the soldiers during which women hand out white feathers to men out of uniform for being cowards. After being taught the basics of cooking by Mrs Patmore, Sybil leaves to do nurse training in York. Branson, while driving her there, reveals he has fallen in love. Bates is forced to leave after Vera threatens to expose the story of Mary and Kemal Pamuk, implicating Anna. Anna is broken-hearted but believes he is hiding something from her. Violet is exposed as having tried to exclude William and Molesley from conscription under false pretences. Daisy kisses William – and quickly regrets it. Thomas, in the Medical Corps, has his hand shot, so that he can return home.

Episode Two ▲
Directed by: **Ashley Pearce**
Written by: **Julian Fellowes**

April 1917. Anna thinks she has spotted Bates in the village. Matthew returns to England briefly for a recruitment drive for soldiers. Mary invites newspaper tycoon Sir Richard Carlisle to dinner; Matthew and Lavinia attend. Rosamund discovers that Lavinia and Carlisle share a secret. Carson is ill; when Mary goes to see him, he tells her to let Matthew know how she really feels. Mary says goodbye to Matthew at the station as he returns to the front, just stopping short of telling him she still loves him. The blind soldier that Sybil and Thomas have cared for at the village hospital kills himself. Under Isobel's influence, the family decides to turn Downton Abbey into a convalescent home for officers. Edith is seen kissing Farmer Drake by his wife, so loses her war work driving the tractor on the farm. William prepares to leave for the front and asks Daisy to be his sweetheart. Carlisle proposes to Mary.

Episode Three ▲
Directed by: **Andy Goddard**
Written by: **Julian Fellowes**

July 1917. The house is now a convalescent home for officers, with the family reduced to the small library and dining room for their own private quarters. Thanks to O'Brien's manipulation of Cora, Thomas is promoted to Acting Sergeant in order to run this hospital outpost, putting him effectively in charge of Sybil (as nurse) and above Carson. Matthew has a few hours' leave and returns to Downton Abbey. Anna hears that Bates is working in a pub – The Red Lion in Kirkbymoorside – and goes to find him there. General Sir Herbert Strutt comes to dinner and Branson attempts to pour a tureen of slop over him but is caught in time by Carson. Lang, Robert's new valet, is dismissed; his shellshock has rendered him unfit for work. William and Daisy get engaged, much to his delight and her unease. Robert asks Matthew to take William as his servant at the front.

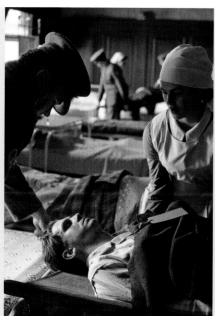

Episode Four ▲
Directed by: **Brian Kelly**
Written by: **Julian Fellowes**

1918. Mary overhears Branson telling Sybil that he knows she's in love with him and confronts her about it. Mary accepts newspaper baron Sir Richard Carlisle's proposal. Isobel and Cora clash over who is in charge of the house. Isobel decides to go and work for the Red Cross at the front. Mrs Bird, her cook, and Molesley start a soup kitchen out of Crawley House for begging soldiers. Mrs Patmore and Daisy find out and help them. William and Matthew go missing in action. Robert goes to see Bates at the pub to ask him to return to the house. Molesley is disappointed – he had been preparing to step into Lang's shoes as valet. Mrs Hughes discovers convalescing officer Major Bryant and housemaid Ethel in an empty bedroom in the servants' attic – Ethel is sacked on the spot. The officers put on a concert, to boost morale. As Mary is singing 'If You Were The Only Girl In The World', Matthew walks back in and joins in the song. Ethel returns and tells Mrs Hughes she is pregnant.

Episode Five ▲
Directed by: **Brian Kelly**
Written by: **Julian Fellowes**

August 1918. Amiens, France. There is an explosion – William covers Matthew with his body, Matthew is thrown onto a rock. The force of the blast fatally injures William's lungs. Violet pulls strings to have William moved from Leeds Infirmary to Downton Abbey. O'Brien writes to Vera Bates to tell her that her husband has returned to the house; Vera turns up and says she is going to sell the story of Kemal Pamuk to the papers. Tipped off by Anna, Mary asks for Carlisle's help to stop her. Matthew is told by Dr Clarkson that he may never walk again. Mrs Hughes gives food to Ethel and her baby; Bryant does not wish to acknowledge his child. Jane, a war widow, begins work as a housemaid at Downton. Robert begins to feel excluded as Cora is so busy. Carlisle announces his engagement to Mary in the paper, much to everyone's surprise. Daisy reluctantly marries William on his deathbed.

Episode Six ▲
Directed by: **Andy Goddard**
Written by: **Julian Fellowes**

November 1918. The war is coming to an end. Patrick Gordon arrives as a badly burned officer, claiming to have a connection with the family. Daisy, wearing a black armband, is distressed by having misled William on his deathbed. Mary looks after Matthew, who is in a wheelchair – he has asked Lavinia to leave as he doesn't want her burdened. Mary and Carlisle go to look at Haxby Hall with a view to buying it. Violet tries to find a new cause for Isobel, who has returned from the Red Cross. Bryant is killed in the final battle of the war. Robert comes down to the servants' hall to announce the end of the war. Carson decides to accept Carlisle's invitation to go and work for him and Mary at Haxby Hall. Carlisle and Cora plot to bring Lavinia back. Bates receives a telegram telling him his wife Vera is dead.

Episode Seven ▲
Directed by: James Strong
Written by: Julian Fellowes

April 1919. The house is restored back to normal. Thomas decides to go into the black market business. Carlisle asks Anna to spy on Mary for him – she refuses and tells Carson. Major Bryant's parents come to the house for lunch; Ethel interrupts to break the news about their grandson, Charlie, but they do not believe her. Matthew unexpectedly recovers from his injury and announces that he and Lavinia will marry just as soon as he can walk down the aisle. Violet tells Matthew that Mary is still in love with him. Bates hears from his lawyer that a letter Vera wrote has been discovered, saying Bates was coming over and that she was afraid for her life. Sybil leaves a note to say she's on her way to Gretna Green; Mary knows it is with Branson. Edith, Mary and Anna pursue them and find them staying in a public house on the road; they take Sybil home. Thomas's venture is a failure; he was tricked and has lost every penny he had.

Episode Eight ▲
Directed by: James Strong
Written by: Julian Fellowes

April 1919. Tom and Sybil announce their engagement in the library. Tom (now he is going to marry Sybil, he is no longer known as 'Branson') has been offered work as a journalist in Dublin. Robert tries to pay Tom off with a cheque. Carson is ill and has to stay in bed. Molesley steps in to serve the wines at dinner but gets drunk on 'tasting' them. Cora retires to bed feeling ill and is nursed by O'Brien. Lavinia also goes pale and retires to bed – the wedding is postponed. Matthew and Mary dance in the hall – they kiss and are seen by Lavinia. With so many off sick, Thomas steps in to help as footman. The Bryants offer to take Charlie on condition Ethel never sees him again – she says no. William's father writes to Daisy and asks her to go to his farm. Lavinia takes a sudden turn for the worse, and dies. Bates and Anna marry at the register office in Ripon. Robert kisses Jane; she hands in her notice. Bates is arrested for murder.

Episode Nine ▼
Directed by: Brian Percival
Written by: Julian Fellowes

Christmas 1919. Bates is in prison. All the family are staying at the house, including Robert's sister Rosamund and Carlisle. Daisy finds a planchette board in the back of a cupboard. Rosamund's lady's maid, Shore, causes trouble. Violet invites Sir Anthony Strallan for tea with her and Edith, only to discover he has lost the use of an arm. Lord Hepworth, a fortune hunter, comes to stay for the shoot on New Year's Day with Rosamund. Sybil writes from Dublin to say that she's pregnant. Lavinia Swire's father has died. Mary admits to Matthew that Carlisle is getting on her nerves. At Bates's trial O'Brien, Mrs Hughes and Robert are called as witnesses for the prosecution. Bates is sentenced to death for wilful murder. Robert is told about Mary and Pamuk: he tells her to weather the scandal and not marry Carlisle. Isobel tells Matthew that Mary is still in love with him. Thomas hides Robert's dog Isis and then tries to 'find' her in order to win Robert's gratitude. Daisy goes to see Mr Mason at the farm. Bates is reprieved from his death sentence. On 12th January they have the Servants' Ball. Daisy asks for promotion to under cook. Rosamund finds Hepworth and Shore in bed together. Matthew proposes to Mary in the snow and she accepts.

SERIES THREE

Episode One ▼
Directed by: Brian Percival
Written by: Julian Fellowes

Spring 1920. Everyone is preparing for Matthew and Mary's wedding. O'Brien wants her nephew, Alfred, to be the new footman. Robert hears from his lawyer Murray that he has lost his fortune in a single bad investment. Anna is determined to find evidence that proves Bates's innocence. Edith rekindles her romance with Strallan. Matthew tells Molesley he won't be moving him to the big house as his valet. Daisy goes on strike. Sybil and Tom are sent money for the fare by an anonymous donor, so they can come to the wedding. Matthew is told that he is one of three possible heirs to Reggie Swire's vast fortune; he tells Mary he won't take the money. Thomas and Carson refuse to be Tom's valet when he is at the house. Lord Merton and his sons come to dinner; one of them, Larry Grey, spikes Tom's drink. Cora's mother Martha Levinson arrives and makes a dramatic entrance. Matthew is relieved to see Mary arrive at the church for their marriage.

Episode Two ▼
Directed by: Brian Percival
Written by: Julian Fellowes

1920. Matthew and Mary arrive back from their honeymoon to the news that Downton is going to be put up for sale. Thomas takes revenge against Alfred for being promoted to valet. Isobel has a new cause; rescuing 'fallen women'. Ethel turns up. Robert persuades Strallan to call off his romance with Edith; but she won't accept the decision. Violet and Mary plot to get more money out of Martha. Mrs Hughes discovers a lump in her breast. Matthew inherits Reggie Swire's fortune but still won't accept it. Anna finds Vera's friend Mrs Bartlett – she could hold the clue to Vera's death. Molesley is reinstated as Matthew's valet. A planned grand dinner turns into an indoor picnic after the kitchen range breaks down. Alfred kisses Martha's maid, Reed.

Episode Three ▼
Directed by: Andy Goddard
Written by: Julian Fellowes

The day of Edith's wedding approaches. The family have a picnic at Eryholme, where they may move to when the house is sold. Thomas lies to Molesley that O'Brien is leaving, and Molesley mentions it to Cora, much to her surprise. Tom gives in and wears a dinner jacket. Bates is warned that he is going to be set up by his cellmate Craig. Anna goes to see Mrs Bartlett, to find out more about Vera. Swire has left Matthew a letter; it says that he knew Lavinia had tried to call off the wedding and asks him not to hold back from enjoying the money because of any 'grief, guilt or regret'. Matthew tells Robert that he is going to give him Swire's money. Robert refuses but they decide to become joint masters of the estate. Strallan jilts Edith at the altar. Mrs Hughes finds out that her tumour is benign; Carson sings with happiness.

Episode Four ▲

Directed by: **Andy Goddard**
Written by: **Julian Fellowes**

August 1920. Mary encourages Matthew to get into the detail of how the estate is run. Anna reveals that she's had no letters and not been allowed to see Bates for some time. Ethel has written asking to meet Mrs Hughes; she wants the Bryants to have Charlie after all. Tom turns up in the middle of the night. He has fled Dublin, suspected for being involved in the arson of Anglo–Irish homes in Ireland. He has left a heavily pregnant Sybil behind and Robert is furious. Mrs Hughes has bought herself an electric toaster. Jimmy, the gorgeous footman, is taken on. Sybil finally arrives. O'Brien plants the seed of making Thomas think Jimmy likes him. After seeing off his cellmate, Craig, Bates is given all of Anna's letters in one big batch. Anna receives all of Bates's letters. Edith's letter to *The Times* is published. Ivy, the new kitchen maid, starts work.

Episode Five ▼

Directed by: **Jeremy Webb**
Written by: **Julian Fellowes**

Sybil is in labour. Sir Philip Tapsell, a London expert, is brought in. Anna goes to visit Bates to discuss her meeting with Mrs Bartlett; they realise that Vera cooked a pie with poison to set Bates up. Isobel takes Ethel on as a housemaid. The editor of *The Sketch* has asked Edith to write a weekly column. Mrs Bird resigns on the appointment of Ethel because of her former work as a prostitute. Daisy is harsh with Ivy. The labour is not going well – Sybil's ankles are swollen and she is getting muddled. Clarkson and Tapsell disagree over treatment for Sybil. The baby is born safely but Sybil has a fit hours later, and dies. Thomas is dropping hints to Jimmy, making him uncomfortable. Murray comes to talk to Anna about the new evidence for Bates. Matthew puts his foot in it, asking him about the estate when everyone is in a state of grief. Cora blames Robert for Sybil's death.

Episode Six ▲

Directed by: **Jeremy Webb**
Written by: **Julian Fellowes**

Sybil's funeral has taken place. Tom announces that their baby daughter, also named Sybil but always referred to as 'Sybbie', will be christened a Catholic. Ethel asks for Mrs Patmore's help to cook a lunch. Isobel asks Cora, Edith, Mary and Violet to lunch; Carson is apoplectic that they will be cooked for by someone who used to be a streetwalker. Mr Mason tells Daisy he'd like to leave the farm to her. Violet persuades Dr Clarkson to tell Cora and Robert that even if he had operated as he had wanted, Sybil might not have survived. Bates blackmails Craig – he is to force Mrs Bartlett to change her statement. Robert is upset about Matthew's criticisms over the running of the estate. Jimmy is getting increasingly uncomfortable with Thomas's intimate gestures. Daisy teaches Alfred how to dance the foxtrot. Mrs Bartlett gives a new statement to Murray; Bates will be freed.

Episode Seven ▲
Directed by: David Evans
Written by: Julian Fellowes

Bates is released from York prison. Matthew has a meeting with Jarvis, the land agent. Bates and Anna are given a cottage on the estate. Matthew worries he is infertile. Thomas goes into Jimmy's room when he's asleep and Alfred bursts in on them. Edith goes to meet the editor of *The Sketch*, Michael Gregson, in his office and then for lunch at Rules the next day – he wants her to be a columnist. Tom's brother Kieran comes to stay and Tom has to force him out of the servants' hall. O'Brien encourages Alfred to tell Carson what he saw. Sybbie has her Catholic christening. Robert and Mary, under the influence of Violet, decide to appoint Tom as the estate's new land agent.

Episode Eight ▼
Directed by: David Evans
Written by: Julian Fellowes

1920. Bates is reappointed as Robert's valet. Carson suggests to Thomas that he resign. It's the village cricket match. O'Brien tells Jimmy to push the case against Thomas. Violet's eighteen-year-old niece, Lady Rose MacClare, comes to stay. Matthew and Tom start drawing up new plans for the estate. Bates discovers that Thomas is being asked to leave without a reference and decides to help him. Rose goes to London with Mary and Edith and is discovered having a fling with a married man. Mary and Matthew discover each other at the fertility doctor's clinic. Edith, who has been falling in love with Michael Gregson, discovers that he is married; he explains his wife is in an asylum so legally he cannot divorce her. Ethel leaves to work in the same village as the Bryants and Charlie. Thomas is promoted to under butler; Jimmy is promoted to first footman. The police turn up at the cricket match looking for Thomas – Robert sees them off.

Episode Nine ▼
Directed by: Andy Goddard
Written by: Julian Fellowes

One year later. September 1921. The Crawleys are off to Scotland, to Duneagle, to stay with their cousins and Rose's parents, Lord and Lady Flintshire (Shrimpie and Susan) for ten days. Michael Gregson is also visiting the area and joins them. Mary is heavily pregnant – she has a month to go. Tom stays behind at Downton where the new maid, Edna, sets her sights on him. A grocer, Joe Tufton, makes deliveries to the house; he flirts with Mrs Patmore. Anna asks Rose for reeling lessons before the Ghillies' Ball. At the fair in Thirsk, Jimmy is saved from thugs by Thomas and Dr Clarkson almost proposes to Isobel. Molesley gets drunk at the ball. Edith decides not to give Gregson up. Mary feels unwell and decides to go home early – she has the baby. Matthew gets off the train to see them before driving back to the house – he is killed by a lorry.

SERIES FOUR

Episode One ▲
Directed by: **David Evans**
Written by: **Julian Fellowes**

It's six months since Matthew died – Mary and Isobel are still deep in mourning. Tom encourages Mary to take an interest in the farm – Robert is more reluctant. O'Brien has left suddenly to work for Susan MacClare. Mrs Hughes tries to encourage Isobel to help rescue Mr Grigg, Carson's former music hall partner, who is now in the York workhouse. Thomas notices that Nanny West is neglecting Sybbie and reports her to Cora. Edna sees Rose's advertisement for a lady's maid in the post office. Daisy uses an electric whisk to make mousse. Violet asks Molesley to help out at a lunch to encourage Lady Shackleton to hire him but her butler Spratt thinks he's after his job and trips him up. Edith meets Gregson at the Criterion in London. He tells her he loves her. Ivy likes Jimmy and thinks he's sent her a Valentine's card – but he's sent it to Lady Anstruther. Daisy thinks Alfred sent her a Valentine's card until Mrs Patmore admits she sent it. Mary joins the tenant farmers' lunch.

Episode Two ▼
Directed by: **David Evans**
Written by: **Julian Fellowes**

Former maid Edna starts work as Cora's lady's maid – she and Thomas recognise kindred spirits in each other. A letter is found in Matthew's things that indicates he wished Mary to be his sole heiress, should anything happen to him. Molesley admits to Anna he hasn't worked since Matthew died and now he owes money all over the village – Bates finds a way to help him. Rose asks Anna to accompany her to a dance for farmers and servants in Ripon. Carson reveals that his anger with Mr Grigg was over a woman he loved, Alice Neal. Thomas gets the blame put onto Anna for a burn mark on Cora's shirt. Gregson tells Edith he will live in Germany, so that he can divorce his wife. Jimmy has got tickets to take Ivy to the theatre in Ripon. Murray confirms that Matthew's letter is legally binding and Mary owns half the estate.

Episode Three ▼
Directed by: **Catherine Morshead**
Written by: **Julian Fellowes**

Lord Gillingham arrives with his valet, Green. There's a house party but Tom is unhappy to be dressed in white tie and feels out of place – Edna stirs things up with him again. Dame Nellie Melba is coming to sing – Carson and Robert think she should eat on a tray in her room, which angers Cora. Mrs Patmore falls ill so Alfred helps out with the sauces. Molesley is working as a delivery boy for the grocer's so Carson asks him to help out as footman. A guest, Sampson, fleeces everyone at cards. All the servants, even the kitchen staff, are permitted to hear Dame Nellie Melba sing. While watching the singing, Anna goes downstairs to get a pill for her headache and is raped by Green. Edna gives Tom large whiskies; they go to bed together. Gregson wins all the money back from Sampson, which pleases Robert.

Episode Four ▲
Directed by: **Catherine Morshead**
Written by: **Julian Fellowes**

Anna is bruised and shaken – she can hardly bring herself to talk to Bates. Edna tells Tom that she may be pregnant. Alfred hears the Ritz is setting up a training school for cooks. Jimmy flirts with Ivy, upsetting Alfred. Rose, Mary, Gillingham, Tom and Rosamund go to the Lotus Club. When Rose's dance partner runs off to be sick, the band leader – Jack Ross – steps in. Tom confesses to Mrs Hughes about Edna. Bates presses Anna to find out what's wrong. Gillingham pursues Mary and proposes. Gregson gives legal authority to Edith over his affairs. Edith succumbs to a night with him, and is ticked off by her aunt the next morning. Mary turns Gillingham down – she's still in love with Matthew. Thomas suggests a candidate to replace Edna.

Episode Five ▲
Directed by: **Philip John**
Written by: **Julian Fellowes**

Baxter. Cora's new lady's maid, arrives with her electric sewing machine. Thomas knows something about her past that she wants to keep a secret. Mary wants to evict the Drewes, tenant farmers who haven't paid the rent – Robert offers to lend them the money to pay off the arrears. The engagement is announced between Gillingham and Mabel Lane Fox. Anna still won't tell Bates what's happened. Dr Clarkson asks Isobel to help him find work for a man, John Pegg – she gets him a job as a gardener for Violet. She later accuses him of stealing a paper knife. Edith hasn't heard from Gregson since he went to Germany. Alfred does a test at the Ritz but doesn't win a place. Carson's offer of a job as footman for Molesley is withdrawn. Thomas wants Baxter to keep him informed of gossip from the family and other servants. Edith goes to see a doctor in Harley Street. Bates confronts Mrs Hughes over what's wrong with Anna – she tells him Anna was raped but that a stranger broke in and did it.

Episode Six ▲
Directed by: **Philip John**
Written by: **Julian Fellowes**

Evelyn Napier comes to stay, with his colleague, Charles Blake. Tom and Mary have decided to start intensive farming with pigs. Rose plans a surprise for Robert's birthday. A netsuke goes missing from Violet's desk. She suspects Pegg and dismisses him – Isobel goes on the warpath. Cora's brother, Harold, is in trouble and asks for Robert's help. Gregson has vanished. Alfred hears that he has got a place at the Ritz, after all. Daisy is upset and believes Ivy has driven him away. Bates and Anna decide to have a night out. The maitre d' of the hotel refuses to seat them until Cora steps in. Jimmy kisses Ivy but tries to take it too far. Carson reluctantly gives the job of footman to Molesley; everyone agrees he will still be called Molesley not Joseph. Jack Ross's band is the surprise for Robert's birthday dinner. Mary goes downstairs to pay Jack and sees Rose kissing him.

Episode Seven ▲
Directed by: Edward Hall
Written by: Julian Fellowes

Robert is leaving for America to help Harold. Bates doesn't want to leave Anna, so Thomas is given the opportunity to travel with him instead – after Mrs Hughes admits to Mary what has happened. Violet is unwell – Isobel nurses her to prevent the bronchitis turning into pneumonia. Isobel encourages Tom to go to a political meeting in Ripon, where he meets the village school teacher Sarah Bunting. Edith is forced to admit to Rosamund that she is pregnant but that she will 'get rid of it'; when she gets to the clinic she can't go through with it. Rose and Jack go boating in Kensington Gardens. Mary and Blake go to inspect the new pigs and discover that they are severely dehydrated – they spend hours into the night, giving them water and getting very muddy in the process. Gillingham comes to stay – he and Blake know each other from the war – and so Green is back in the servants' hall. Mrs Hughes lets Green know she knows.

Episode Eight ▼
Directed by: Edward Hall
Written by: Julian Fellowes

Summer, 1922. Robert is in America helping Harold deal with the Tea Pot Dome Scandal. Farmer Drewe is asked to manage the pigs for the estate. Rosamund tells Cora that she and Edith are going to Switzerland for a few months to perfect their French – Violet guesses Edith's secret. Alfred proposes to Ivy in a letter – she refuses him. Tom sees Rose and Jack having tea in Thirsk – he tells Mary. Gillingham stays again, with Green – Anna worries that Bates suspects him. Rose tells Mary she is going to marry Jack. Anna goes to London with Mary; Bates asks if he can go to York on the same day. Tom rescues Sarah Bunting at the roadside. Isobel meets Lord Merton at Violet's luncheon. Mary goes to see Jack – he tells her he won't marry Rose. Baxter and Molesley get more friendly. Mary asks Gillingham to sack his valet but doesn't tell him why. Gillingham tells Mary he has broken his engagement with Mabel Lane Fox. Robert comes home just as the bazaar begins in the Downton Abbey grounds. Gillingham arrives to tell Mary that Green is dead. Daisy sees Alfred and wishes him well as a friend. Blake admits to Mary that he can't stop thinking about her.

Episode Nine ▼
Directed by: Jon East
Written by: Julian Fellowes

Summer, 1923. The household is in London for Rose's coming out ball. Edith returns from Switzerland, having weaned the baby. Martha and Harold are over from America. At the Embassy Club, Sampson steals a letter from the Prince of Wales that is in his mistress's bag – Rose feels responsible. Tom stays behind at the house. Sarah Bunting asks to be shown round and they are seen by Thomas, who suspects the worst. Mrs Hughes collects clothes for Russian refugees – Anna donates an old coat of Bates's. Mrs Hughes discovers a train ticket to London for the day Green was killed – Baxter sees her. Mrs Hughes gives the ticket to Mary, who throws it in the fire. Harold's valet asks Daisy if she will come to America to be his sweetheart and to cook for Harold; she says no but Ivy asks to go as cook instead. At Rose's ball, the Prince of Wales arrives and asks her for the first dance. Gillingham reveals that Blake is heir to a baronetcy and one of the largest estates in Ulster – battle commences for Mary's hand. Edith hears that Gregson has been in a fight with the Brownshirts. She is regretting leaving her daughter with a family in Switzerland – she meets Farmer Drewe who agrees to take the baby on. The servants have their outing – a day at the beach. Carson and Mrs Hughes hold hands and paddle in the sea together.

SERIES FIVE

Episode One ▼
Directed by: Catherine Morshead
Written by: Julian Fellowes

1924. The Labour Party is in government. Daisy grumbles that there's no kitchen maid to replace Ivy. Lord Merton is pursuing Isobel. There's a proposal for a war memorial in the village; Carson is asked to be the chairman of the committee, much to Robert's consternation. Gillingham and Sarah Bunting come to Robert and Cora's thirty-fourth wedding anniversary dinner. Lady Anstruther, Jimmy's former employer, invites herself to tea and ends up staying the night. Molesley dyes his hair black – it is not a subtle look. Mrs Hughes finds Gregson's German primer in the guest bedroom and gives it to Edith. Daisy tries to educate herself but is frustrated. Thomas suspects that Baxter knows something that links Bates to Green's death. Molesley persuades Baxter to tell Cora her story, rather than let her hear it from Thomas. Edith sobs over Gregson's book as she lies in bed; then accidentally throws it into her fire, setting the room alight. Gillingham suggests to Mary that they go away together for a week. Jimmy is discovered in bed with Lady Anstruther and is sacked.

Episode Two ▲
Directed by: Catherine Morshead
Written by: Julian Fellowes

There is disagreement over where to site the war memorial – Robert wants it in the village, Carson wants a garden on the site of the cricket pitch. Jimmy leaves. Molesley is now the only footman. Edith goes to see her daughter, Marigold, at the Drewes'. Mary asks Anna to go to the pharmacy to buy her a contraceptive device. Rose persuades Robert to get a wireless to hear the King's speech. Mrs Patmore hires Miss Bunting to give Daisy lessons. Thomas tells Molesley that Baxter stole from her previous employer. Simon Bricker, the art historian, comes to dinner to see the painting by Piero della Francesca. Blake acknowledges he has lost the battle for Mary, but doesn't seem too upset about it. Mary checks in to the Grand Hotel, Liverpool for a week with Gillingham.

Episode Three ▲
Directed by: Catherine Morshead
Written by: Julian Fellowes

Mary and Gillingham are at the hotel together; he is keen they marry quickly. Violet's butler, Spratt, sees them leaving – and tells Violet. Violet pretends they were there for a conference. Daisy is encouraged by her lessons with Sarah Bunting. Sergeant Willis interviews Bates – a witness to Green's death has come forward. Mrs Patmore hears that her sister's village is refusing to add her nephew's name to the memorial because he was shot for cowardice. Thomas asks for time off because his father is ill. Cora decides Baxter can keep her job. Cora feels Robert doesn't take her opinions seriously. Mary asks Anna to hide the contraceptive with the Marie Stopes book in her cottage. Bricker takes Cora out for dinner in London – Robert is furious. Mrs Drewe is irritated by Edith's attention to Marigold. Tom is thinking about going to America. Rose holds a tea for the Russian refugees at Downton. Violet meets Prince Kuragin again – they have a past.

Episode Six ▼
Directed by: **Philip John**
Written by: **Julian Fellowes**

Edith hears definite news that Gregson is dead. There's a point-to-point at Lord Sinderby's house, Canningford Grange. Blake and Gillingham are riding – Mary decides to join them. Denker, Violet's new lady's maid, starts work. Thomas looks worse and worse; he begs Baxter for help. Bates discovers Mary's contraceptive device in the cottage and confronts Anna. Violet goes to see Kuragin – he is still in love with her. Sergeant Willis interviews Baxter. Edith has inherited Gregson's publishing company. Isis isn't well. Mary has her hair cut to a bob. Carson and Mrs Hughes go with Mrs Patmore to see the cottage she decides to buy to run as a bed and breakfast. Bates admits to Anna that he considered going to London on the day Mr Green was killed but didn't in the end. She realises they have destroyed the proof of his innocence – the train ticket was unused. Edith decides to leave and take Marigold with her – Mrs Drewe is distraught. Carson suggests to Mrs Hughes that they might buy a property together.

Episode Four ▲
Directed by: **Minkie Spiro**
Written by: **Julian Fellowes**

Violet and Isobel go to visit Kuragin in York. Lord Merton proposes to Isobel – he has fallen in love with her. Thomas has returned – Baxter discovers him with a box of syringes in his room. Mary and Rosamund go to a fashion show in London – they see Blake who introduces Mary to Mabel Lane Fox. Molesley is feeling overworked as 'first footman'. Shrimpie comes to stay; he is divorcing Susan and tells Rose. Bricker comes to stay – Robert is not pleased. Mary breaks up with Gillingham but he refuses to accept it. Daisy and Mrs Patmore are summoned to the dining room to give their view on Miss Bunting's lessons. There's a huge row and Robert asks Miss Bunting to leave and never return. The police discover Anna went to the spot where Green died when she was in London with Mary.

Episode Five ▲
Directed by: **Minkie Spiro**
Written by: **Julian Fellowes**

Mrs Patmore has been left some money by an aunt and asks Carson for investment advice. Sergeant Willis comes to talk to Anna and Lady Mary. Violet recruits Dr Clarkson to prevent Isobel's marrying Lord Merton. Tom calls it a day with Sarah Bunting – she decides to accept a job with a school in Preston. Rose's new beau is Atticus Aldridge; he is the son of Lord Sinderby, a pillar of the Jewish community. Drewe tells Edith to stay away from Marigold completely or they'll leave the farm. Blake sets up lunch with Mary and Mabel. Violet and Rosamund suggest Marigold is sent to a school in France. Bricker comes to the house again to photograph the painting and goes to Cora's room in the night – Cora does not welcome him. Robert finds them when he comes home unexpectedly – he and Bricker have a punch-up.

Episode Seven ▼
Directed by: **Philip John**
Written by: **Julian Fellowes**

There's a house party, with Rosamund, Gillingham, Blake, Mabel, Lord Merton, the Sinderbys and Atticus. Cora discovers Edith's secret from Mrs Drewe. Molesley tries to encourage Daisy to go on with her education. Gillingham admits he is better suited to Mabel but he feels he cannot be the one to give Mary up. Lord Sinderby is not keen on the idea of his son and Rose getting married. Isobel announces her engagement to Lord Merton but after his son Larry Grey reveals his anger, she breaks it off. Tom has written to his cousin in Boston to ask his advice on moving out there. Cora persuades Edith to return and tell Robert that she has taken pity on Marigold, so she is able to join Sybbie and George in the nursery. Blake and Mary stage a kiss so that Gillingham finishes with her once and for all. Atticus proposes to Rose. Robert and Cora go to bed with the dying Isis between them.

Episode Eight ▲
Directed by: **Michael Engler**
Written by: **Julian Fellowes**

Everyone is going to London for Rose's wedding. Shrimpie and Susan are to pretend they are happily married for the duration – Lord Sinderby disapproves of divorce. Tom's cousin has asked him to go to Boston to be his business partner; he decides he will leave after Christmas. Anna is asked to go to Scotland Yard – she is identified in a line-up and arrested. Kuragin proposes to Violet. Atticus is set up by Susan at his stag party; compromising photos of him are sent to Rose. Daisy is taken to the Wallace Collection by Molesley and Baxter; her eyes are opened and she decides to hand in her notice to work in London. Robert decides to sell the della Francesca so that they can restore the tenants' cottages. Denker arrives back completely drunk from a night out at a gambling den with Andy, a temporary footman – Andy has lost all his money. Thomas goes with Andy and Denker to the gambling den and wins Andy's money back for him. The war memorial is unveiled, together with a small stone for Mrs Patmore's nephew. Robert realises that Marigold is Edith's daughter. Daisy decides not to leave after all. Rose and Atticus are married.

Episode Nine ▲
Directed by: **Minkie Spiro**
Written by: **Julian Fellowes**

Autumn, 1924. Mary goes to see Anna in prison in York. Lord Sinderby has rented Brancaster Castle from Lord Hexham for a shooting party. Mrs Hughes and Carson discuss houses they're going to buy but she admits she has no money. Violet reunites Kuragin with his long-lost wife who Shrimpie has tracked down. Lord Sinderby's butler, Stowell, is snobbish to Tom. Thomas decides to take him down a peg. Robert tells Edith he knows about Marigold. Atticus has been offered a job in New York. House guest, Charlie Rogers, arrives in a smart car bringing a friend, Henry Talbot – Mary stands by him for the shoot. Edith dances with Bertie Pelham, the estate's land agent. Sinderby's mistress and love-child turn up, having been invited by Thomas as part of his plan to get back at Stowell – Rose covers for Lord Sinderby. Bates writes letters of confession – everyone knows they are just to get Anna out of prison – and goes on the run to Ireland. Baxter and Molesley prove his innocence by finding the landlord of a York pub who remembers seeing him that day. Robert has an ulcer. The della Francesca has sold well. Carson hires Andy as the new footman, Carson buys a house and tells Mrs Hughes he has registered it in both their names. Carson proposes to Mrs Hughes – she accepts. Bates returns.

SERIES SIX

Episode One ▲
Directed by: **Minkie Spiro**
Written by: **Julian Fellowes**

1925. The new year and the local hunt meets on the Downton drive. Violet is outraged by the news that the Royal Yorkshire County Hospital wants to take over Downton Cottage Hospital. Mary is blackmailed by a maid from the hotel in Liverpool where she stayed with Lord Gillingham. Edith's maid has left to work in a shop in Ripon. Tom is settled in Boston; Rose in New York. Mary makes a decision about her future. Denker breaks a confidence. Mr Mason receives some unwelcome news. Mrs Hughes is nervous about Carson's expectations of marriage.

Episode Two ▲
Directed by: **Minkie Spiro**
Written by: **Julian Fellowes**

There's discussion about where Carson and Mrs Hughes should hold their wedding reception. Daisy is worried about Mr Mason. Battle lines are drawn over plans for the hospital. Thomas is worried about his future. Edith battles with the editor of *The Sketch*. Mary suggests an outing for the children. Anna tells Mary about her difficulties starting a family – Mary takes her to her doctor in London. The family have a fright at the Malton Fat Stock Show.

Episode Three ▼
Directed by: **Philip John**
Written by: **Julian Fellowes**

Mrs Hughes hasn't chosen a dress for her wedding — Anna and Mary hatch a plan. Violet is on the warpath. Thomas has a realisation. Daisy is hopeful that Mr Mason's problem will be solved. Spratt is concerned about a relative. Molesley helps Daisy with her studies. Edith sacks her editor. Cora visits the York hospital. On the day of the wedding there's a surprise for everyone.

Episode Six ▼
Directed by: **Michael Engler**
Written by: **Julian Fellowes**

Downton Abbey is to be open to the public for a day. Daisy is preparing for exams. Dr Clarkson receives news about the village hospital. Tom and Mary go to London. Thomas spends time with the children. Molesley gets an unexpected offer. Mrs Patmore overhears a conversation that makes her jump to the wrong conclusion. Larry Grey's fiancée extends the hand of friendship to Isobel. Baxter receives a letter that leaves her shaken.

Episode Four ▲
Directed by: **Philip John**
Written by: **Julian Fellowes**

Carson and Mrs Hughes go on honeymoon. Violet invites Lady Shackleton to dinner – she brings her nephew. Sergeant Willis comes to see Baxter. Mary finds a cottage on the estate for the Carsons. Cora has a suggestion about the estate farms, but Mary doesn't agree. Anna is worried. Mary goes out to supper in London. One of Rosamund's lunch guests is a familiar face. The servants' hall is decorated for the return of Mr and Mrs Carson.

Episode Five ▲
Directed by: **Michael Engler**
Written by: **Julian Fellowes**

Tom considers his future. Violet invites the Minister of Health, Neville Chamberlain, to dinner. Thomas's attempts at friendship are rebuffed. Carson and Mrs Hughes have their first supper in their cottage. Edith interviews for a new editor. Denker causes trouble at the Dower House.

Episode Seven ▲
Directed by: David Evans
Written by: Julian Fellowes

Mrs Patmore's bed and breakfast is open for business. Mrs Hughes confesses she does not enjoy cooking for Carson in their cottage – she has a plan to improve things at home. Isobel is invited to Larry Grey's wedding. Thomas disappoints Carson. The family and servants go to a car race at Brooklands. Mary has to make a difficult decision, which angers Violet. Violet has a gift for Robert.

Episode Eight ▶
Directed by: David Evans
Written by: Julian Fellowes

Rosamund counsels Cora and Robert to reveal Edith's secret. Sergeant Willis comes to tell Mrs Patmore some bad news. Molesley's future is looking brighter. Baxter makes a shocking discovery. Violet and Mary have a heart-to-heart. Mary makes trouble for Edith. There is good news for Thomas. The identity of *The Sketch*'s agony aunt is revealed.

313

Afterword

BY GARETH NEAME

So that's it then. Our camera has pulled away from Downton Abbey for the last time and we have left the characters to continue their lives, for better or worse, but certainly in very different circumstances from when we first met them in 1912. We will never know what fate lies in store for the estate and how Mary and then George will weather the storms of the post-war era. When George inherits the title, will he end up having to make a deal to bring Downton into state ownership or will he make a good fist of it all, continuing the modernising trend established by his parents and uncle, and preserve Downton, just as Highclere Castle itself has survived?

We always set out to depict these characters as being much more like us than different from us, despite the ninety years that separate our age from theirs. Indeed Sybbie, George and Marigold could still be alive today. That's assuming George survives the Second World War, in which he will presumably serve. As I say, we really will never know what becomes of them all. And that's probably the thing I shall miss the most.

But Downton is fiction. It merely represents a way of life that existed. And so many of us are connected to that world – the British fans at least. Many of our ancestors would have worked in service, which was a significant source of employment for generations. We are a people that sit comfortably with our past and most of us live within a short drive of a historic house such as Highclere Castle. Indeed visits to Lanhydrock House in Cornwall, and specifically its kitchens and servants' quarters, captured my imagination before I was even considering the territory for a television show.

Many fans of *Downton Abbey* have visited Highclere Castle and the village of Bampton in Oxfordshire. The show has also taken us to locations as far afield as Inveraray Castle in the Scottish Highlands, Alnwick Castle in Northumberland and Basildon Park in Berkshire. But whether you live in Britain or plan to visit from abroad, there are hundreds and hundreds of beautiful and historic places in the UK to explore and enjoy.

We wanted the show to combine fast-paced and narrative-packed storytelling with the finest production values. Our locations, sets and costumes are lavish, our directors and actors renowned. And perhaps it is this combination, the *re-booting* of a much loved genre for the twenty-first century, that has proved so popular.

Downton Abbey can be seen in 250 territories worldwide and if it is hard to quantify exactly what that means, it is essentially everywhere it is possible to sell television content. Combined with the awards recognition – fifty-nine Emmy nominations and eleven wins at the time of writing, together with victories at the Golden Globes, the Screen Actors Guild, a BAFTA Special Award and many others – it is perhaps Britain's most successful scripted television export ever. That success is the result of *Downton* entertaining so many people, all around the world.

These achievements were all made possible by the creative genius of Julian Fellowes and the instinctive and smart decision-making by those who backed us from the outset – Peter Fincham, Laura Mackie and Sally Haynes at ITV, together with our US partner Masterpiece on PBS and our studio NBCUniversal International. The show's iconic home was only established due to the hospitality and support of the Earl and Countess of Carnarvon. But most of all, it has been down to our extraordinary cast of much-loved actors, and the talented and committed directors and crew. *Downton Abbey* has been marshalled from the outset by my friend and partner Liz Trubridge, together with Nigel Marchant and Chris Croucher. A dream team if ever there was one.

A final word about Jessica Fellowes. Her inspiration is her own love and affection for the show and she has served it so well over the years. Together with the sumptuous work of our photographer Nick Briggs, this book is the ultimate memento of the last six years.

GARETH NEAME *August 2015*

THE DOWNTON ABBEY CAST

Hugh Bonneville	The Earl of Grantham (Robert)	**Jonathan Jaynes**	Postmaster
Elizabeth McGovern	The Countess of Grantham (Cora)	**Nicky Henson**	Charles Grigg
Maggie Smith	The Dowager Countess of Grantham (Violet)	**Cathy Sara**	Mrs Drake
		Brendan Patricks	Evelyn Napier
Michelle Dockery	Lady Mary Crawley	**Theo James**	Kemal Pamuk
Laura Carmichael	Lady Edith Crawley	**Fergus O'Donnell**	Farmer Drake
Jessica Brown Findlay	Lady Sybil Crawley	**Bill Fellows**	Joe Burns
Lily James	Lady Rose MacClare	**Bernard Gallagher**	Bill Molesley
Jim Carter	Mr Carson	**Robert Bathurst**	Sir Anthony Strallan
Phyllis Logan	Mrs Hughes	**Sean McKenzie**	Mr Bromidge
Brendan Coyle	Mr Bates	**Jane Wenham**	Mrs Bates
Robert James-Collier	Thomas Barrow	**Christine Lohr**	Mrs Bird
Joanne Froggatt	Anna Bates	**Richard Hawley**	Sergeant
Allen Leech	Tom Branson	**Amy Nuttall**	Ethel Parks
Thomas Howes	William Mason	**Zoe Boyle**	Lavinia Swire
Matt Milne	Alfred Nugent	**Maria Doyle Kennedy**	Vera Bates
Siobhan Finneran	Sarah O'Brien	**Cal Macaninch**	Henry Lang
Kevin Doyle	Mr Molesley	**Iain Glen**	Sir Richard Carlisle
Penelope Wilton	Isobel Crawley	**Lachlan Nieboer**	Edward Courtenay
Sophie McShera	Daisy Mason	**Jeremy Clyde**	General Robertson
Lesley Nicol	Mrs Patmore	**Daniel Pirrie**	Major Bryant
Dan Stevens	Matthew Crawley	**Paul Copley**	Mr Mason
Raquel Cassidy	Phyllis Baxter	**Clare Calbraith**	Jane Moorsum
Ed Speleers	Jimmy Kent	**Michael Cochrane**	The Reverend Mr Travis
Tom Cullen	Tony Gillingham	**Tom Feary-Campbell**	Captain Smiley
Julian Ovenden	Charles Blake	**Julian Wadham**	General Sir Herbert Strutt
David Robb	Dr Clarkson	**Trevor White**	Major Gordon
Michael Fox	Andy	**Christine Mackie**	Mrs Bryant
Samantha Bond	Lady Rosamund Painswick	**Kevin R. McNally**	Mr Bryant
Shirley MacLaine	Martha Levinson	**Sharon Small**	Marigold Shore
Jeremy Swift	Mr Spratt	**Nigel Havers**	Lord Hepworth
Sue Johnston	Miss Denker	**Nick Sampson**	Prosecution barrister
Matthew Goode	Henry Talbot	**Simon Poland**	Defence barrister
Harry Hadden-Paton	Bertie Pelham	**Timothy Carlton**	Judge
Rose Leslie	Gwen	**Cara Theobold**	Ivy
Charlie Cox	Duke of Crowborough	**Lucille Sharp**	Reed
Jonathan Coy	George Murray	**Jason Furnival**	Craig
Helen Sheals	Mrs Wigan	**Charlie Anson**	Larry Grey

Douglas Reith	Lord Merton
Sarah Crowden	Lady Manville
Neil Bell	Durrant
Mark Penfold	Mr Charkham
Clare Higgins	Mrs Bartlett
Michael Culkin	Archbishop of York
Tim Pigott-Smith	Sir Philip Tapsell
Terence Harvey	Jarvis
Charles Edwards	Michael Gregson
Ruairi Conaghan	Kieran Branson
Richard Teverson	Dr Ryder
Edmund Kente	Mead
Edward Baker-Duly	Margadale
Nigel Harman	Mr Green
Gary Carr	Jack Ross
MyAnna Buring	Edna Braithwaite
Di Botcher	Nanny West
Harriet Walter	Lady Shackleton
Moray Treadwell	Farmer at tenant farmers' lunch
Nigel Betts	Farmer at tenant farmers' lunch
Andrew Alexander	Sir John Bullock
Kiri Te Kanawa	Dame Nellie Melba
Patrick Kennedy	Terence Sampson
Joanna David	Duchess of Yeovil
Joncie Elmore	John Pegg
Andrew Scarborough	Tim Drewe
Yves Aubert	Arsene Avignon
Simon Lowe	Maitre d'
Daisy Lewis	Sarah Bunting
Paul Giamatti	Harold Levinson
Poppy Drayton	Madeleine Allsopp
James Fox	Lord Aysgarth
Oliver Dimsdale	Prince of Wales
Janet Montgomery	Freda Dudley Ward
Emma Lowndes	Mrs Drewe
Richard E. Grant	Simon Bricker
Naomi Radcliffe	Mrs Elcot
Anna Chancellor	Lady Anstruther
Patrick Brennan	Mr Dawes
Rade Sherbedgia	Prince Kuragin
Christopher Rozycki	Count Rostov
Howard Ward	Sergeant Willis
Peter Egan	The Marquess of Flintshire (Shrimpie)
Catherine Steadman	Mabel Lane Fox
Matt Barber	Atticus Aldridge
Louis Hilyer	Inspector Vyner
James Faulkner	Lord Sinderby
Penny Downie	Lady Sinderby
Ed Cooper Clarke	Tim Grey
Phoebe Nicholls	The Marchioness of Flintshire (Susan)
Alun Armstrong	Mr Stowell
Jane Lapotaire	Princess Irina
Sebastian Dunn	Charlie Rogers
Alice Patten	Diana Clark
Nichola Burley	Rita Bevan
Adrian Lukis	Sir John Darnley
Patricia Hodge	Mrs Pelham
Rick Bacon	Mr Henderson
Martin Walsh	Mr Finch
Trevor Cooper	Mr Moore
Paul Putner	Mr Skinner
Ronald Pickup	Sir Michael Reresby
Victoria Emslie	Magazine secretary
Philip Battley	John Harding
Rupert Frazer	Neville Chamberlain
Antonia Bernath	Laura Edmunds
Phoebe Sparrow	Amelia Cruikshank
Noah Jupe	Child at open house
Fifi Hart	Sybbie
Oliver & Zac Barker	George
Eva & Karina Samms	Marigold